DRUMS THROU

Charles L. White

IT IS THE OBJECTIVE of this small volume to acquaint the reader with some of the ancient and modern instruments of percussion, and at the same time present glimpses of intriguing relevant matter which they suggest; for in the pageant of music and sound, variety seems to have no end. No less truly, drums and percussion offer infinite ways of expressing not only rhythm and harmony, they likewise show patterns of culture and paths to civilization. By association they divulge a history of mankind and perhaps even of Earth.

THE BOOK IS DESIGNED not only for drummers. It is for all who are interested in Music and its appreciation: for Music Lovers, for Music Instructors and Music Majors. For Arrangers, Composers, Conductors, Managers, Critics, Librarians. For those intrigued by the relevant, and for all who lean toward the humanities.

Through parallels in evolution, this unusual book tells of Drums being discovered or invented by primitive man-animals before they could talk intelligibly. It points out how the musical development of the human infant is a facsimile of that of the whole human race over vast periods of time. It is a book for those interested in primitive man, both past and present. It is a book for the scientist as well as for the artist.

CHARLES L. WHITE

THE AUTHOR. For over forty years he has been tympanist of the Los Angeles Philharmonic Orchestra and for many years a faculty member of the School of Music, University of Southern California. During these years Mr. White realized that almost everyone who walks near his drums has an impelling urge to touch them. This universal primitive desire aroused the thoughts which eventually led to this book. *Photo by Otto Rothschild.*

DRUMS THROUGH THE AGES

DRUMS THROUGH THE AGES

First Printing

THE FOLLOWING EXCERPTS:

From *A Treatise on Modern Instrumentation and Orchestration,* by Hector Berlioz, translated by Mary Cowden Clarke. Copyright, 1882, by Novello & Co., Ltd., London. Reprinted by permission of Novello & Co., Ltd. From *The Travels of Marco Polo (The Venetian),* revised from Marsden's Translation and Edited with Introduction by Manuel Komroff. Copyright, 1926, by Boni & Liveright, New York. Reprinted by permission of Boni & Liveright. From *Genghis Khan,* by Harold Lamb. Copyright, 1927, by Harold Lamb. Reprinted by permission of Doubleday & Co., Inc., New York. From *From The Hunter's Bow,* by Beatrice Edgerly. Copyright, 1942, by G. P. Putnam's Sons, New York. Reprinted by permission of Beatrice Edgerly.

Library of Congress catalog card number: 60-53596.

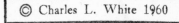

DRUMS
THROUGH THE AGES

The Story of our Oldest and Most Fascinating
Musical Instruments

By CHARLES L. WHITE

Illustrated by George DeBeeson

1960
THE STERLING PRESS
LOS ANGELES, CALIFORNIA

Table of Contents

38294

CHAPTER I

Da Capo — An Introduction

A BOOK dealing with the instruments of percussion would be incomplete and without foundation if it did not include some reference to their origin and development. Most of the few books on the subject state merely that in retracing the history of musical instruments, the thread is lost in the unfathomable depths of ages long gone. It is not difficult, however, by means of comparison, to trace the Drum back to its source in the dim prehistoric past — back to the time when mankind played drums, but had not yet learned to talk.

To point the way and clear a path for a journey taking us many thousands of years into the past, we have only to ask the help of those great men who already have made extensive investigation in the realm of Science, and then correlate their observations with the natural tendencies shown in the musical development of the average child of today, as it follows the evolutionary patterns disclosed by Haeckel and Gregory.

The writings of travelers and explorers of the eighteenth and early nineteenth centuries also are of immense value in reconstructing long forgotten days. The great work of Mary E. and William Adam Brown, collecting primitive instruments from all over the world, together with information relative to their construction and use, and then cataloguing the results of their research in "Musical Instruments and Their Homes" has, like Percival Kirby's "Musical Instruments of the Native Tribes of South Africa," provided a key of inestimable worth to the study of instruments and music. Browns' book cannot fail to call attention to a marked similarity in the first drums found by early explorers in widely separated parts of the world. The study of languages discloses in them certain likenesses which have survived even to the present day; and the fact that some natives from one part of the world may understand and converse with some other natives from an entirely different region, though they never before have met, further emphasizes a basis for the theory of a common origin not only for Drums, but, by inference, for Man himself.

Gregory, in "Our Face from Fish to Man," has dealt with the antiquity of mankind by means of the evolution of the human skeleton. He has traced this evolution through fossils recorded geologically since the beginning of life on our planet, and his discoveries have been correlated with those of Haeckel, in the field of embryology. Many other investigators have provided additional pertinent and convincing information regarding the development of Early Man, and of his environment and habits.

The following excerpt from Hugh Miller's "Old Red Sandstone" may prove to be of interest to the reader who pursues the relevant: There exist wonderful analogies in nature between the geological history of every mammifer, — between the history, too, of fish as a class, and that of every single fish. "It has been found by Tiedemann," says Mr. Lyell, "that the brain of the foetus in the higher class of vertebrated animals assumes in succession the various forms which belong to fishes, reptiles, and birds, before it acquires those additions and modifications which are peculiar to the mammiferous tribes." "In examining the brain of the mammalia," says M. Serres, "at an early stage of life, you perceive the cerebral hemispheres consolidated, as in fish, two vesicles isolated one from the other; at a later period you see them affect the configuration of the cerebral hemispheres of reptiles; still later, again, they present you with the forms of those of birds; and finally, at the era of birth, the permanent forms which the adult mammalia present." And such seems to have been the history of the vertebrata as an order, as certainly as that of the individual mammifer. The fish preceded the reptile in the order of creation, just as the crustacean had preceded the fish, and the annelid the crustacean. Again, though the fact be somewhat more obscure, the reptile seems to have preceded the bird. . . .

In a similar manner the evolution of the music of the race from savagery to civilization may be seen through the development of music in the individual from infancy to adulthood, for both follow the same pattern. The musical progress of the individual during a single lifetime is a condensed version of that of the whole race during countless ages of time.

Changes in the structural form of mankind have been traced back to the lowly slipper animalcule and jellyfish of Palaeozoic Times by means of fossils. Through embryology the development of the individual is shown to be a complete panorama of the development of the race, beginning as a cell and then progressing through the various stages required during eons of time to produce, by evolution, a human race. The *child* recapitulates in its mental and physical development from infancy to adulthood what the *race* has attained over vast periods of time. And just as the development of the human race may be followed through the development of the individual, so may the development of the Music of the race be observed by studying the musical development of the average individual.

Fortunately, for the sake of comparison, there still are living on Earth many primitive peoples whose musical habits are known; and there are also many human infants and children whose musical progress may be surveyed at will.

To summarize the beginning and early development of musical instruments and music, and to look so far back into the past as to predate the period during which mankind learned to walk in an upright position and before he could talk intelligibly, it is necessary only to base our conclusions on what we know of primitive man, past and present, what we are shown in the evidence disclosed by embryology and palaeontology, and simply watch the musical progress of the average child of today.

A new-born babe cannot talk. Primordial man could not talk. The ability to talk depends upon the muscles of the tongue, which are inserted in the chin tubercles, certain bony processes, and the motive power located in the brain. The existence of these is lacking in the non-speaking animals, and also in the oldest known specimens of human skulls. Articulate speech requires that the brain be sup-

plied with the third or lowest convolution in the frontal
lobe, as therein resides the directive power needed to
move the muscles of the tongue, and this third convolution
was not incorporated into the brain of those of our human
ancestors who were first upon Earth.* From this we may
infer that primitive man was *unable* to talk until after the
Creator had furnished him with the tubercles, muscles, and
processes pertaining to the chin and tongue, and with the
third convolution in the frontal lobe of the brain with which
to control their use. We may, therefore, establish a parallel
situation with a child before it has *learned* to talk. So,
with the help of a child and our knowledge of primitive
peoples, their instruments and customs and the facts established by Science, it is possible to reconstruct the
musical scene of ages past, and to more fully understand
and appreciate our present-day instruments, music and
musicians.

*Colbert, Humanity in its Origin and Early Growth.

THE DESIRE to make sounds of a rhythmic or musical
nature appears very early in life, both in the race and in
the individual. This desire, or instinct, is characteristic
not only of the human family, but it is well represented in
many of our fellow creatures. Certain birds, though unable
to sing, are said to *drum* when they make their typical
rhythmic noises. Surely everyone has heard "the deep
woods resound with the thunderous *drumming* of the ruffled
grouse." Other birds, the songsters, produce vocal music
that is variously beautiful and charmingly melodic. Many
bugs are enthusiastic musicians. Perhaps the first music

of the ancient world was the shrill stridulations of the aboriginal insects who lived during the Cretaceous period, seventy- to ninety-millions of years ago.*

*Charles L. Camp, The Earth Song.

The Stridulations of the Insects, or what *might* have been. The first musical impulses to be felt by any of the creatures of Earth were those experienced by the stridulating insects of the Cretaceous period, seventy- to ninety-millions of years ago. Had there been suitable musical instruments available at that time, it is easily imaginable that the insects might have played upon them when they followed the instinctive musical urge placed in them by Nature. Having no instruments, however, —not even the washboards nor the little brown jugs of the hillbillies— these primitive musicians utilized what there was at hand: their own bodies, legs, or wings.

When Raymond Lee Ditmars, the famous zoologist, was a boy, he noticed the musical traits of the orthopterous insects, and, with the youthful enthusiasm that later led him to fame, he experimented with their natural musical ability. His first collection of six-legged artists was of the katydid family.* Young Raymond found several of these primitive musicians, each of whom fiddled in a different key; but his repeated attempts at organizing them into an orchestral ensemble always failed completely, for when one insect played, the others became polite, put down their fiddles and bows, and attentively listened.

Many of our backyard visitors still retain the musical inclinations implanted by Nature in their ancestors millions of years ago, and such unique violinists as cone-head grasshoppers, locusts, black crickets, katydids, and (the most proficient instrumentalists of them all) the pale-green snowy tree crickets, enjoy their musical impulses and, weather permitting, scrape out endless concerts on the balmy night air.

Like the Malayan watchman, who signals an alarm by clicking on his bamboo slit-drum, these friendly insects utilize their musical talent for such a purpose, too — only in reverse. In the Orient, crickets are often kept as household pets, in which capacity they serve as watchdogs; but instead of sounding an alarm on their crickety violins when an intruder enters, the insect ensemble stops fiddling immediately, as if some great maestro had rapped his stand, and the sudden burst of silence awakens those who have been sleeping.

*Edwin W. Teale, Boys' Book of Insects.

The wings of the female orthopterons are not usually equipped with the front wing-covers which provide the "fiddle and the bow," so it is only the male crickets who qualify to play in this all-morache police band, or in our summer evening backyard concerts.

Homer, the great writer of the Iliad and the Odyssey, spoke of the *song* of the cicada. This ancient grasshopper-like insect does not have to resort to fiddling or drumming to express itself in music, for Nature has provided it with a "voice-box" at the base of its abdomen. The real drummer among the bugs, however, is a small beetle which makes its home in the seasoned woodwork of old houses through which it burrows. This insect imitates the beating of drumsticks, in perhaps what might be called the very first rudiments of rudimental drumming,* by beating its head against the walls of its abode. It does not play a continuous sequence of notes, but patterns its exercises more nearly like the separate beats of smaller configurations. A certain species of ant scrapes the hard surface of its abdomen against the dry leaves of its nest, in order to play its primitive morache-violin. The locust merely rubs its wings together when answering the urge to communicate or to make music. The insects in the nearby bush, or the tiny water-bugs in the babbling brook may be heard

---

*The history of Rudimental Drumming dates back to the year 1758, when Charles the First of England willed and commanded that "all drummers within ye kingdome of England and ye principalitie of Wales" play marching beats exactly alike. The various beats were eventually standardized and developed into twenty-six different patterns, and these became known as the "Rudiments" of drumming. — Charles L. White, Beginning Percussion for Teachers and Students.

merrily clicking their joy at being alive, if there are interested ears to listen closely.

By means of the musical tones of his reeded pipe, the charmer lures snakes from their nest. Nature has not provided these slender reptiles with music-making equipment; but, nevertheless, snakes seem to appreciate and enjoy those harmonious sounds which are said to wash away from the soul the dust of everyday life.

Going back again into pre-history we are both reminded and assured that sound and rhythm have been a form of expression since almost the very beginning of geologic time, for even fishes are said to express themselves by means of recurring sounds. Croakers, drumfish, and many other varieties have this primitive musical ability, this urge to create sounds. It is said to be true even of whales.

A word of clarification may be needed about the *sound* that whales make, for all whale sounds are not necessarily of a musical nature.

". . . There she blows! – there she blows! There again – there again!" So we read in the story of Moby Dick, the White Whale. . . . "He's going to *sound!* In stunsa'ls! Down top-gallant-sa'ls! Stand by three boats. . . . "

In this case the *sound* a whale makes is not to be confused with its quasi-musical primitive grunting, for when a fish or whale is 'sounding,' it is diving for the bottom.

LEGENDS, records and other evidence show conclusively that drums are extremely ancient in origin. The sacred legends of the Maoris of New Zealand and those of the Karens of ancient India tell of the Drum being invented by pre-human anthropoids, whom, for want of a more accurate name, they called *monkeys*.

According to the stories handed down by the Karens of primitive India, monkeys were the makers of the first drum. In their legends about the Monkeys and the Drum,* the tale concerns a farmer, Mr. Pa Maw Taw, whose home and rice paddies were on the side of a beautiful lofty mountain, near the top of which was a large cave inhabited by monkeys. Mr. Taw was one of the earliest ancestors of the Karen people. He lived so long ago that the generations of men who have lived since his time could not be counted on the fingers and toes of many people.

One year, after working hard in the paddies and bringing his crop of rice almost to the very eve of a successful harvest, Pa Maw Taw had more than his share of trouble with his neighbors, the monkeys. Every day they came and ate the ripening grain, and then stole all they could carry to their cave. Every day "P.M." chased them away, but they were too much for him to bear. Finally, one day when he was very tired, disgusted and discouraged, Pa Maw Taw just gave up. He was completely worn out both physically and mentally. In his dispair he thought he would lie down in the soft shade of a nearby banyan tree and try to think of some scheme which might help him get rid of the pests.

Being so tired and so disheartened, Mr. Taw fell asleep

*Sadis N. Coleman, The Drum Book.

soon after lying down. When cautiously he awoke, the monkeys were gathered around him. They thought he had died, so "P.M." let them think that such was the case. He pretended to be dead, just to see what would happen.

One large monkey, who seemed to be the leader of the group, spoke at last. "We have been most unkind to our Karen neighbor, Mr. Pa Maw Taw," he said in a sad voice. "We have eaten his best rice and we have carried much of it away to our cave for the winter, and we have made no effort to pay him for it. Our most unworthy actions have made this poor soul unhappy. Our treatment of him has caused his untimely death, and it is our duty to give him a funeral with rites suiting one of such commendable hardworking habits and fine personal character." Several of the monkeys then gently lifted Mr. Taw from the ground, and slowly carried him to the top of the mountain, where they placed him at the mouth of their cave.

After they had carefully laid him down, some of the monkeys went into the cave to get their instruments, for to them a funeral was not considered adequate unless it was accompanied by the beating of drums.

"P.M." was peeking out of one very thin eye. To him it was an interesting adventure.

At last the monkeys returned with a large drum made of solid silver. Then others came with one of silver and gold combined, and inlaid with emeralds and rubies. It was carried by a shimmery rope made of braided cobra skins, and beneath the drum was an elaborate stand of carved ivory which was formed into the shape of a huge rampant scorpion. Then the final group of monkeys brought their favorite pure white, shining drum, which they had named "Gaw Wa." As soon as all the drums were assembled and the drummers were in readiness, a signal was given and the monkeys began beating lustily, in accordance with the rites and traditions of the ancient monkey-people.

The funeral ceremony was well under way. The drums beat a boisterous clamor while the repentant monkeys marched sorrowfully around the recumbent Mr. Pa Maw Taw, wishing for him a happier life in the next world. In the midst of the solemnities, Pa Maw Taw, whom they thought surely was dead, had a tickle in his nose, so he suddenly sat up and sneezed! This so badly frightened the monkeys that they fled in terror to the other side of the mountain, without bothering to take their treasured drums with them. They never returned to their cave again, so Mr. Taw took the fascinating beautiful drums to his grass-roofed home near the cool green rice paddies down the mountainside, and during leisure hours he and his friends admired the drums and learned many things about them. But at last, alas, they were stolen from him and were never seen again. Fortunately, however, having the monkeys' drums to copy from, the ancient Karen people were able to build their own instruments. And that, it is said, is how drums were first introduced into India.

Maori legends call the ancient drum-makers the "first people" and state that they were descendants of non-hairy monkeys.* These "first people" had no language, but they are said to have invented the drum. Hindu epic poems state that the anthropoid apes had almost human attributes. They

*Ettie A. Rout, Maori Symbolism.

talked with a language of their own; they sat in council
with the Hindus; they formed armies and fought together'
with the Hindus. They were intelligent. But as time went
on, the apes deteriorated both physically and mentally until they became as we know them today.*

According to the tales handed down from the ancient
people of Mexico, and recorded in the Sacred Book of the
Quiche Maya, "Popul Vuh," a marvelous being called
Quetzalcoatl, or sometimes Huemac, appeared in Mexico
from the East (Atl-antis) soon after giants had disappeared
from the land and the ceasing of earth tremors made habitation possible for the human beings who came to live on
Earth. With him, Quetzalcoatl brought civilization, learning
and rules for moral conduct. When, however, those whom he
tried to help refused to benefit from his teachings, Quetzalcoatl returned to the mysterious land in the East. He proph-
esied that the world would be destroyed by hurricanes, and
that mankind would be changed into monkeys – *all of which
came to pass long ages ago,* if we are to believe the legends
of the Aztecs.

Thomas N. Savage, M.D., wrote in the Boston Journal of
Natural History (1847) that the natives of Equatorial West
Africa believe the anthropoid apes were once members of
their own tribe; that for their depraved habits they were
formerly expelled from all human society, and that "through
an obstinate indulgence of their vile propensities, they
have degenerated into their present state and organization."

The legends of the Karens, Maoris, Hindus and Aztecs
seem to warrant a possible higher estate for our anthropoid
*The Ramayana.

cousins, the "monkeys," at some time in the distant past. And the primitive natives of Equatorial West Africa are not alone in their beliefs concerning the apes, for the thought has long been advanced that savage races are not really 'primitive,' but that they are the degenerate remnants of a former civilization, of which the apes are the most degraded. Biological studies show that apes are more human-looking when they are born than when they die; they seem to become more animal-like, more bestial, as they advance from ape infancy to ape adulthood.*

Today these ancient drum makers may be regarded culturally as being far below the most backward human tribe. But today, if we wish a glimpse that far back into the hazy mists of antiquity and pre-civilization, we need only visit the zoo and watch the gorilla and the chimpanzee, and note that they have this ancient inborn desire to make more-or-less rhythmic sounds by clapping their hands together, by beating their chests, and by pounding or slapping on logs or trees. They are quite proficient in shaking rattles, too.

*G. de Purucher, Studies in Occult Philosophy.

TRULY we may say "In the Beginning there was Rhythm." For aeons before the most rudimental of musical instruments were possible of construction, or even thought of, there was Rhythm. Nature has expressed Rhythm since Time began, and continues to do so on every hand. The great and small cycles, the years, the seasons, day and night, the tides, electricity, the beating of the heart, and even life and death follow a rhythmic pattern. History is said to repeat itself: another form of Rhythm. It is no wonder then that mankind responds to this compelling urge to express itself rhythmically either in sound, which we call 'Music,' or in motion, which we call 'dancing.' Music is said to be the combination of *harmonious* tones, or melody, with Rhythm. Rhythm, even without harmony or melody, is capable of great power and charm; but without Rhythm, harmony and melody are but senseless, chaotic, unmanagable sound. Without Rhythm there could be no great symphony orchestras, for any form of ensemble playing would then be impossible.

In examining the development of the primitive races at present on Earth, there has been found but one tribe of aboriginees so backward that they possessed no music whatever. Another tribe was found being able to count only to five, but it had already 'invented' the drum and had incorporated its use into the routine of the lives of its people.

Before he is able to walk or talk, the average child of today will have found pleasure or satisfaction in producing sounds by striking objects together. Before the child has learned to clap his hands and play pat-a-cake, he will have done considerable banging of spoon on dish or furniture. Some day, probably long before he has spoken his first word, that wonderful being he will learn to know as Mother will mysteriously place in his hands his first musical instrument: a rattle made of rubber or plastic. In a similar manner, soon after he had discovered the pleasure of making recurrent sounds by striking sticks or stones together, or by clapping his hands, Mother Nature gave to Early Man a similar instrument: a rattle made of a seed-filled gourd.

Both primitive man and today's child are comparative:

each advances slowly with his musical education. In common they continue the hitting-on-something and shaking-the-rattle stages for a considerable time, laying the ground-work for that very important part of Music: Rhythm. They both are quite young. They have yet to learn to walk in an upright position and to speak a language well enough to be understood, and by the means of which to convey their thoughts. Undoubtedly the child will be true to form both as an individual and as a summary of the racial development in Music through the ages.

After the bang and rattle urge become less pronounced, a child will experience instinctive desires felt by primitive man. He will want to perform on the notched stick (morache) or on the notched gourd (guiro); but not having access to these instruments, the modern primitive will probably scrape a stick along a picket fence, or place a cardboard or a piece of paper in the spokes of his bicycle in order to produce a similar sound. He will experience the desire to possess a drum with heads of skin, and to make delight-fully loud rhythmic noises on it, as well as to accomplish the feat of making it 'roll' and produce a sound like that of a briskly shaken rattle. He will have discovered the use of a knife during this period, and with its help he will make whistles from the branches of certain trees, or from the stems of suitable grasses; and in due sequence he will no doubt resort to a tin whistle or an harmonica, for he must have his Pipes of Pan.

Boys and girls now may begin their musical education in a more up-to-date way, but any modern instrument upon which they choose to play will be but the descendant of the prim-

itive instruments of their own, and of humanity's infancy
and childhood.

The discovery of a tablet pertaining to the ancient colon-
ization of Egypt led the noted archaeologist, Paul Schliemann, to explorations which ultimately threw interesting
light on prehistoric musical instruments. The record in-
scribed on the tablet, which was discovered at Maycarne,
on the island of Crete, stated that the first Egyptians were
Atlanteans headed by Thoth, the god of Writing and History,
and that they settled at Sais, a wild uninhabited place on
the eastern Nile delta, about 14,000 B.C., in order to escape the wrath of King Cronas of Atlantis, whom the priest,
Thoth, had displeased. The tablet stated further that the
first temple of the Egyptians was built by Thoth at Sais,
and this led to the archaeological project of unearthing it
by Dr. Schliemann.

In his report relative to discoveries made during five
months of excavating the ruins of the ancient temple, Dr.
Schliemann notes that among other interesting archaeological finds was a burial chamber containing a collection of
musical instruments and also a papyrus, as yet undeciph-
ered, but which was believed to be an unknown kind of
Egyptian musical scoring. The hieroglyphic inscription on
the sarcophagus stated that the collection of musical instruments was that of the temple, and that it was used in
the coronation of Amenemhat I, in which participated sixty-
five musicians and a chorus of eighty voices.

Most of the instruments were made either of wood or por-
celain, although one horn was of a brass-like metal. There
were harps with strings made from human hair, and other

instruments fashioned from human bones.

A closing remark by Dr. Schliemann in his report claimed that in his various excavations he found that the older Egypt was, the more cultured it was, and that the nation simply degenerated after Atlantis vanished.*

According to the writings of the oldest known historians of Greece and Egypt, the final submergence of Atlantis occurred about 9600 years before the birth of Christ. While this date does not agree with the period claimed by Schliemann to have witnessed Egypt's greatness and decline, there is no reason to doubt that the civilization which produced the musical instruments he discovered was one of great antiquity. And long before such instruments as he reported could have been thought of and built, humanity must have progressed through many ages of time — unless it appeared on Earth fully developed mentally and physically, possessing at its very beginning all the knowledge and culture of a mature civilization. Being that this seems hardly probable, mankind must have developed musically much after the human pattern itself.

*Col. James Churchward, The Children of Mu.

The Skeleton of a Prehistoric Andean Drum.

CHAPTER II

Sticks and Stones

NATURE has incorporated into mankind as a race, and into man as an individual, a desire to make sounds by means of *striking* objects together in a more or less rhythmic manner. Another desire implanted in man is to *shake* various objects which produce rattle-like sounds; while yet another is to create ratchet-like sounds by means of *friction*.

The *desire* to beat, shake and scrape the numerous primitive instruments found or invented by early man, and the pleasure he derived from their crude sounds of incipient music, led to the development of the first instruments of percussion and then to the other instruments which have followed.

Our very first instruments were just plain sticks and stones. "The natives of West Australia accompany their dances by clapping their hands and stamping their feet." "The natives of Central Australia accompany theirs by beating two pieces of stick together, or two green branches." The same has been said of the Adaman Islanders. The natives of Africa "strike sticks or fagots together with the greatest of energy." In the southwestern United States, the Indians wove their drums into basket form and played on them with their two hands, which they clapped together occasionally while playing. Sometimes they beat on their basket-drums with two sticks, which they struck together at intervals as part of their music, thus clearly associating the beating of the drum with the clicking of the sticks, or with the clapping of hands.

The mountainous islands which form the last outpost of the Andean chain, before it sinks into the sea at Cape Horn, are the habitat of the Yahgan. These aboriginal savages "have no musical instrument at all. Even the rattle, drum and flute are absent" in their musical culture. But the earliest explorers mention that "staves were used to beat time in certain rites." The primitive people of Patagonia, who lived slightly farther to the north, and who were culturally more advanced than the Yahgan, "used a kettle-drum." Their clothing was *painted* on.

Such were the reports of the first explorers to visit among Earth's most primitive and musically retarded people.

The urge to clap hands, to beat upon chests, slap thighs, pound on trees and logs, to strike objects together, is to be seen implanted in all man-like creatures. It is constantly being demonstrated in different degrees of perfection in the woods or jungles, in the zoo, everywhere — even in the nursery at home.

To ancient man any crude sound, even though it might lack rhythmic form and precision, was sufficiently interesting to satisfy his primitive taste and mentality; for to him Music consisted merely of *noise,* and the limitation of being able to create sounds that were either only soft or loud, or fast or slow, in no way disappointed his untrained ear. The sounds of his own making were pleasurable enough for him to enjoy. In due time, however, as man progressed and his

awareness increased, he noticed that some pieces of wood
or stone sounded more vibrant and with a better quality
when struck, than did others; that one stick might produce
a dead, unmusical sound, while another stick or stone
would sound better. In other words, primitive man discovered *resonance*, or *tone*.

After our distant progenitors had become aware of resonance they noticed that besides being more vibrant than
others, some tones were of a different color, that wood and
stone did not sound alike — that each had a different *timbre*.
They noticed that stones and pebbles made sounds that are
short and clicking in character, while certain kinds of wood
have sounds of an entirely different, almost bell-like
quality.

Next to be noticed was that a larger stick or stone had a
deeper tone than did a smaller one, that it had a different
pitch.

The important discoveries of *tone*, *timbre*, and *pitch* led
to our musical scale and eventually to our modern music
and musical instruments. But it took primitive man untold
ages to become mentally aware of their existence, and
clever enough physically to build instruments upon which
he could demonstrate his great discoveries.

From time immemorial to the present day, the sound produced by striking objects together has remained fascinating,
and it is due to this continuity of interest that our modern
percussion instruments have been invented and devoloped.
Ordinary pieces of broken branches, picked up in the jungle
or along the shore, have progressed to become the claves,
xylophone, marimba, wood-block and temple-block. Pebbles

and stones, probably studied more by the primitive men of
the Stone Age, as they chipped and worked with stone and
flint, were our original castanets and cymbals, and the
forerunners of all of the percussion instruments of metal.

THE MUSICAL sounds to be found in Nature, of which there
are eight (according to the Chinese), are those of skin,
stone, metal, baked earth, silk, wood, bamboo and gourds.
Nature provided the materials from which the eight tone-
colors could be made, but left to the choice of man the
responsibility of treating them in the most suitable manner.
From the materials provided by Nature: skin was made into
drums, stone was used for cymbals, metal for bells and
gongs, baked earth was made into horns, silk into lutes.
Wood was made into ideophones such as bells or xylo-
phones, castanets and slit-drums. Bamboo was for flutes
and tuning-pipes, while gourds served as mouth organs.
The Chinese considered drums to be the most important
of all the musical instruments inspired by the gods and
built by men, so they thought there also should be eight
varieties of drums to match the eight kinds of musical
sounds found in Nature. The eight different kinds of drums
made by the Chinese were really very much alike, excepting
in the minor details of size and shape. Drum number eight,

however, combined a secondary sound of Nature with the sound of skin, for it was filled with the husks of rice — which changed the tom-tom into a sort of rattle. Drum number eight had another distinction: it was made in two models — one to be played with the right hand, and one to be played with the left.

To the Chinese, the *sounds* of music, the tone *colors*, are of more importance than the notes into which they may be formed.

BEING MORE easily managable and workable than stone, the original instruments of percussion were undoubtedly of wood. It is quite likely that they were just small sticks for beating together after the fashion of the aboriginees of Africa, Australia, the Adaman Islands, and of the apes and gorillas in the zoo.

Two sticks, similar in shape to boomerangs, are the first instruments recorded by the Ancient Egyptians. These sticks, or clappers, both held in one hand, appear on vases made before 3000 B.C. They resemble the 'bones' of the minstrel show, or those used by small boys of this and other countries.* They are shown in use on an ancient seal excavated from the site of Ur, dated about 2800 B.C. They were used as both a missile and a musical instrument, and they still serve that dual purpose for the natives of Colombia, in northern South America.

The early explorers and travelers of past centuries told

*'Bones' are clappers made from large rib bones. Two are held between the fingers of each hand, and played by a rolling motion of the wrists.

that the simple beating of two sticks together for making music was a common custom among most primitive peoples. When civilization and the slave trade brought the first negroes to the New World, their musical sticks came with them. After sailing from Africa, the first stopping place for the unfortunate slaves was in the West Indies, where their sticks became so rooted in the music of the New World that today they are usually thought of as being of Cuban or Latin origin, instead of having been introduced into the Americas from Africa. The Latin influence of the West Indies has, however, succeeded in translating their name into the Spanish word meaning *sticks,* and now these primitive instruments are generally called *claves.* (cla´-vees)

The sound of the sticks clicking together must have been very fascinating to our first musicians and to many of those who followed, for claves are being struck together in much the same fashion even today. Their shrill staccato tone, due to the hard resonant wood from which they are made, is very colorful and effective when used in suitable music and properly played. From their unsteady beat one might imagine that whoever created the style of playing the claves did not have a good sense of rhythm. The apes and gorillas in the zoo may be seen clapping their hands in a careless,

slipshod manner somewhat similar to the irregular beat of
the claves. This slightly off-rhythm sort of 'Charleston'
beat* must have been a very catchy bit of musical figuration
nevertheless, for all through the long ages of musical development the monotonous little imperfect cadence of the
sticks has never varied. This is the song of the claves:

[handwritten marginalia: imperfect ? bias]

$$\frac{2}{4} \quad \text{♩ ♩ ♩ ♩ ♩ | ♩ ♩ ♩ |}$$

[handwritten marginalia: Comparing the clave to the rythm of Apes + Gorillas?]

It might be written in other ways, but the sound would be
the same:

$$\mathbf{C} \quad \text{♩. ♩. ♩ | ♩ ♩ ♩ | ♩. ♩. ♩ | ♩ ♩ ♩ |}$$

When man's faculties became more developed and alert,
and his sense of hearing became more acute and discrim-
inating, he began experimenting with his sticks. He found
that a better tone could be produced by resting one stick
on the tips of the fingers and thumb and the base of the
palm, cupping his hand so it would form a resonator or
hollow sound chamber beneath it, while he struck it with
its mate held in his other hand.

Having discovered that all sticks do not sound alike in

*The 'Charleston':

pitch, he began building the foundation for the notes of the
musical scale and for melody by making sticks of higher or
lower tones. These he formed into sets consisting of a few
pieces of differently pitched wood. This new instrument
was called 'wood sound,' or *xylophone*.

If we but take a hint from the very beginners in Music of
our own day, we may readily conclude that the first crude
musical instrument, the xylophone, was a three toned one.
We may even put the words to the original song that was
the first bit of melody, for it is still one of the first a child
will sing:

Tom-boy, tom-boy, Suz-ie is a tom-boy

Sometimes the words chosen for this atavistic tune revert
to a primitive 'nyaa nyaa, nyaa nyaa, nyaa nyaa-nyaa nyaa-
nyaa nyaa,' — and sometimes its rhythmic outline varies
slightly in order to fit different languages; but everyone
has heard this youthful song of various lyrics numerous
times in one tongue or another.

The scale of the ancient three-toned flute of the Mayan
Indians used the same intervals:

The two- or three-toned xylophone gradually grew into one
having five tones, and on this greatly improved instrument

many tunes were possible. Some of the melodies suggested by, or made available by the enlarged five-toned scale of the xylophone have lasted through the centuries to the present day. Some are African or Oriental in character; but there are many others with which we should be quite well acquainted, for they range from our lullabies and folk songs to our bugle calls and symphonies. In fact they are so familiar to the American music-lover that the significance of their tonal arrangement is lost.

Striving to obtain more resonance than that afforded by the few crude pieces of wood placed across his legs or resting on two wooden supports as he hit them with a club, primitive man discovered that the tone of his xylophone was increased in resonance and given a different timbre when the bars of wood were suspended by means of a supporting thong strung horizontally through holes drilled across their ends, and then placing hollow gourds beneath them. Thus was the *marimba* invented.

The greatest difference in the two instruments is the hard, glass-like sound of the brilliant xylophone contrasted with the softer, mellow buzzing tones of the thin wide suspended bars of the marimba.

From the first crude beginnings of these instruments having only three and later but five rough sticks placed on two other sticks set over a hole in the ground for resonance, the xylophone and the marimba have developed into attractive and popular modern resonator-equipped instruments of four or more octaves. A large deep-toned *bass marimba* is the latest addition to this branch of the family of percussion.

A Primitive Marimba.

STONES have played an important part in the life and culture of all aboriginal peoples. The Indian considered a stone as a sacred object. Symbolically the sacred stone is round like the universe. It has neither beginning nor end, and it is perfect in itself. It is solely the work of Nature. No artificial means have been used in shaping it. It is composed of only one substance. It is unadulterated. It is genuine, and not an imitation of something else. A stone may not have great superficial beauty; but its structure is solid and durable, like a strong house in which one might safely dwell. So thought the Indian. In the sacred language of the Sioux, the word 'tunkan,' said to be an abbreviation for 'tunkasila,' (grandfather) significantly means both a stone and the moon.*

Stones could be thrown as missiles. Stones lashed to sticks gave the hunter a longer arm and greater strength. The stone arrowhead made man the conqueror of the brute world and the master of less civilized savages.

The men of the Stone Age ground, drilled, chipped and flaked stone, flint, or obsidian. They worked with these materials when making their weapons and implements, and the clicking sounds of ceaseless pounding, chipping and flaking brought an interesting new tone color, or timbre, to their slowly awakening tone-consciousness.

Our earliest musicians found pleasure not only in striking two pieces of wood together; they discovered, too, that

*Frances Densmore, The American Indians and Their Music.

A Primitive Marimba. The early people of southern North America and of Africa learned to improve their xylophone by suspending the bars and placing hollow gourds under them for added resonance.

two pieces of stone struck together like the *po-ha-ku** of the Polynesians, or several small flat pebbles held between the fingers of both hands and clicked together after the fashion of the *ili-ili* of the South Seas, were very pleasant to hear. As they walked along streams or beaches, picking up pebbles to be used as missiles, then thoughtlessly clicking them together, they invented the *castanets*.

The castanets of the Polynesians, *ili-ili*, consist of small pebbles which are held between the fingers and clicked in a manner quite similar to the wooden ones of the Latin races, and the metal ones of the Near East. The *ili-ili* of the Polynesians were our first castanets.

*Po-ha-ku consist of two cylindrically shaped stones similar to claves.

CASTANETS, *'castañuelas'* in Spanish, bear the same name as the *fruit* of the chestnut tree, the *castaña*.

Castanets are similar in shape to the chestnuts after which they are named. Hollowed out for resonance and attached to the player's hands in a manner to allow great facility of execution, the castanets are a most remarkably brilliant member of the percussion family. They are, however, a comparatively recent development of the claves, the clappers, and the ancient cymbals.

According to one writer, castanets were copied after the

finger cymbals of the Ancient Egyptians, which were small, insignificant and toy-like . . . yet which have persisted to this day. He states further that they were not made of brass, but of the wood of the chestnut tree; that they became the characteristic instruments of the Spanish peasantry; and that, "as a mere concession on the part of the South to the bloodlessness of the North," castanets are sometimes mounted on an ebony handle for use in the orchestra.

Another equally well informed writer of music history states that castanets are believed to be of Spanish origin, dating from the immodest dancers alluded to by Martian in his Epigrams. One writer says that the Moors probably adopted them from the Spaniards, while another claims them to have been introduced into Spain by the Moors. It seems likely, however, that the castanets were brought to Spain, the Balearic Islands and to southern Italy by the Phoenicians, for all of these were Phoenician colonies.

In Italy the chestnut tree is called *castagne*. In Thessaly it is known as *kastana*. The similarity in the names seems to suggest a common first source for them. The best early castanets were of Greek manufacture.

The hard reddish-brown wood of the chestnut tree which bears the nuts after which castanets, *castañuelas*, have been named, is a quite suitable material to use for making these effective instruments.

Made of hard wood formed into a shape resembling the rounded, hollowed form of chestnuts, rather than like the flat, spoon-shaped, clapper-like ones previously made, castanets are excellent instruments capable of a wide range of tonal dynamics and almost limitless possibilities of rhythmic technique.

Castanets have been made of many kinds of materials throughout the ages: stone, bone, bamboo, metal, wood. Very hard wood, for whatever variety is used it must be tough enough to withstand the incessant clicking it must endure, yet not so brittle that it will crack or split, and at the same time be hard enough to produce the correct resonance, brilliance and volume of tone. And regardless of what wood may be used in their manufacture, be it chestnut, boxwood, ebony, lignum-vitae, rosewood, snakewood, cocobola, or any other variety, the instruments will still be called *castanets, castañuelas, chestnuts,* not because of the wood of which they are made, but on account of the shape into which they are formed.

Castanets are quite difficult for the percussionist to play properly. If played in the correct Spanish style, held between the thumb and middle finger of both hands, getting the two pairs rapidly into playing position in the limited time usually available is a problem in itself; and the art of manipulating them proficiently requires an immense amount of practice.

When first introduced into the orchestra, the castanets *were* fastened to a handle having a central board for them to beat against; the player simply held the handle and shook it in a manner to conform as closely as possible to the rhythm indicated in the score. This expedient, however, produced a rather uninteresting sound which resembled the dull flapping of clappers more than it did the sharply defined resonant clicking of castanets. Nor could satisfactory precision of rhythm or the necessary expressive shadings be gotten by the shaking technique.

A single pair of castanets mounted on a central handle has a further trait missing in its personality, for it does not possess sex. Like the claves, castanets must have sex, that is, there must be a higher toned one (female) and a lower toned one (male). The lady castanet being played by the right hand, while the left hand plays the gentleman castanet.

INGENUITY AND INVENTION have always been the ally of those feeling the need of anything, so when the desire for castanets having the correct sound and playing possibilities became strong enough, such an instrument was devised. The modern orchestra adaptation of the hand-played *castañuelas* consists of a wooden base upon which are mounted two pairs of properly mated castanets in such a manner as to permit almost as great a facility in technique and expression as could be achieved by playing them in the traditional Spanish style, simply by playing them with the fingers or with soft-headed sticks. The only musical coloration not possible by this convenient arrangement of the instruments being the loud explosive clicks that are produced when two pairs of castanets are struck smartly together.

The brilliant sharpness of the modern hard-rubber castanets is sometimes preferred to genuine instruments made of more expensive hard wood. For the purpose of recording sound, the rubber ones are better on account of their having a higher pitched tone. However, if the proper sound is desired, a male and a female as a pair, care must be taken in selecting those of unequal pitch.

In our country castanets are often used as a signal for elevator operators to start the upward lift of their conveyance, but in Korea one oriental version of this instrument, the *baak,* is used by the conductor of the classical or court orchestra to signal for the music to start, or to stop, or even to signify that a change in tempo is about to take place. The baak is more of a clapper instrument than it is a chestnut-shaped castanet, as it consists of six wooden leaves which are held together by a silk cord at the lower end. These clappers may be folded together like a fan, or they may be held loosely at the bound end and the leaves struck together by hitting the instrument against the player's free hand. This clapper-like castanet, the baak, was invented some 1600 years ago in Song-China, and it was first introduced into Korea during the Goryo Dynasty.

Instruments assigned to similar duties in the Korean classical orchestra are the *chook* (starter) — which is a square box placed on a base, with a wooden hammer or clapper running through the cover — and the *uh* (stopper). The uh, or stopper, is mentioned on page 85 as the *wooden tiger.* In order to stop the orchestra, the conductor scratches the back of this crouching wooden animal with a long piece of split bamboo.

For their castanets, the Japanese use small sections of bamboo. This versatile *grass*, which is chiefly associated with fishing poles in America, has almost unlimited duties assigned to it in the Far East, where it serves as food, floors, roofs, rafts, rafters, posts, walls and waterpipes; furniture, smoking pipes, tools and toys; cooking utensils, life preservers, playing cards, fans; bows and arrows, mats, parasols, baskets, beds, nets, and musical instruments! Bamboo grows in varieties up to one hundred and twenty feet tall, and up to three feet around. It is extremely hard, harder than some metals, and when two small pieces of it are struck together they make a very acceptable click.

Although perhaps more closely related to the claves, these two small pieces of bamboo four or five inches long, one of which is held by the thumb, while the other, held beside it by the fingers, is struck against it, are the castanets of the Japanese.

The Chinese, strange as it may seem — and correctly enough, too — do not consider bamboo a wood. They have made good musical use of this unusual grass, but their neighbors in southeastern Asia have developed this easily adaptable material into an exceptional instrument which is far removed from the flutes, tuning-pipes and ideophones assigned to it by the Chinese. This instrument is the *stamping tube*, or bamboo pipe.

A piece of long-sectioned bamboo, cut just below the joint, the other end open, is dropped or struck with the open up against a solid base, such as hard ground or perhaps a

flat stone. The bamboo used is three or four inches in diameter, and it may be up to four feet in length. The resulting
tone has a vibrant booming quality.

As the length and diameter of the pipes vary, so varies
the pitch of the sounds they produce. When they are tuned
to definite pitches, several pipes are employed to form a
complete melodic instrument. Two of these bamboo pipes
are played by each musician, one held in each hand and
each pipe a different pitch. As several pipes of different
pitch are needed to provide the notes of a melody, several
players also are required to strike the right tone when its
turn comes in the music. It is not considered an ancient instrument on account of the cooperation and teamwork needed in playing it.

The bamboo pipe is thought to be a development of the
primitive stamping sticks used by the early races of Africa
and Polynesia, whose custom was to use a stick, spear or
paddle, to pound vertically upon a resonant object such as
a hollow log, a canoe, or merely a hollowed-out place in
the ground over which flat pieces of wood had been placed.

Stamping tubes made of large-sectioned bamboo, but used
singly instead of in sets, were found generally throughout
most of aboriginal South America.

DESCENDANTS of the stick family of percussion instruments include a wide variety of other instruments, too.
These range in size from a small block of Chinese rosewood
with a narrow slot cut near the top and bottom on opposite
sides, called a *wood-block* and said to be of Chinese origin, to similar drums made of such gigantic proportions

that they require "thirty women to carry them, while the drummers walk beside them shaded by parasols and play this enormous drum."

Drums of this type, with a slot or slit cut into them, are known as *slit-drums*. They are usually placed on the ground in a horizontal position when being played upon. They are common to Africa, Polynesia and America. They are the *lali* of the South Seas, where, as telegraph drums, they may be heard for several miles as messages are sent by means of drum-beats between the inhabitants of neighboring islands.

The *talking drums* of Africa became known in Europe in the early decades of the eighteenth century when Francis Moore described his travels in the Mandingo country of West Africa. Moore found the natives with a talking-drum (tangtang) in almost every village. A century later a similar story was told, but the drum was described as one for *signaling* rather than for *talking*. They were used after the manner of the bugle calls of the Armed Forces. These two reports were interesting for they showed a distinction between drum *talking* and drum *signaling*.*

When H. M. Stanley made his famous journey across Africa in 1875-1877, he traveled through that area of the dark continent in which the talking drums were in general use. Some African tribes still use these drums, which take the place of the telegraph of the West. Messages can be sounded and re-sounded by means of relay drum-stations, until great distances may be covered.

Understanding the messages sent on these unusual drums

*John F. Carrington, Talking Drums of Africa.

requires an understanding of the drum *language*, which is based on the peculiar clicking tongue of the African tribes. Each large tribe has its own individual language, which others do not understand, and there is also a tribal language consisting of high and low clicking sounds which may be imitated on the talking drum. The actual pitch of the sounds is not important. It is the difference between the high soi nd and the low sound which makes the click-language and the similar high or low sounds of the drum understandable.

There are two types of drums used in the African drumtalk. One being of the all wooden slit-drum variety and the other consisting of a pair of large skin-headed drums, one of which has a high tone and the other a low one.

The wooden talking drum of the Belgian Congo is made of a large solid log of hard reddish wood, hollowed out through a long narrow slit cut lengthwise in the log. The wood used is almost always the same, *Pterocarpus Soyauxii,* and the task of making it into a drum is not started until after the log has lain on the jungle floor and begun to rot enough so the tough outer part may more easily be cut away.

The drum-maker first chisels a long narrow slot in the length of the log. The slot is then deepened until it is about halfway through. The inside of the log may then be

An African Talking Drum. The slit-drum has passed beyond the stage of mere resonant tone in the Talking Drums of Africa, for with resonance is combined a high and a low *pitch:* one side of the slot giving a high sound and the other a low one. By playing a series of high and low tones on these drums, the natives are able to converse in the peculiar 'clicking' language they speak, by imitating the high or low sounds of this language on their drums.

An African Talking Drum.

removed by cutting through the slit with a curved ax blade or an adze. The hollowing-out process is done unevenly, so one side of the slit will be hollower and thinner-walled than the other. The hollower, thinner-walled side will give a lower pitched tone when struck than will the thicker side. The two tones, like those of castanets, are distinguished by being either the voice of the male or that of the female; but the lower toned voice of the talking-drum is that of the female, and the high pitched voice that of the male.

The talking-drum is known by various names in different parts of Africa: *bongungu, bongongo, akungu, ngonga.* The word 'gong' means an instrument different from what would now be called a 'drum,' but drums were formerly called *gongs* by widely separated primitive peoples.

Playing on, or talking on the African slit-drums requires no small amount of technique, which the drummer begins learning by diligent practice when a child, on bamboo models built for that purpose. It is not an uncommon sight to see several young aspirants pounding away on large sections of bamboo into which slits have been cut, as they begin learning the language of the drum. They must compose their own signature, too, for each drummer is known by a certain individual beat which no one else may use. The messages sounded are always preceded by the sender's signature, which is repeated at the end of the drumcast.

The drummer, or operator, must be able to place his beats correctly on the high or low side of the slit in order to spell out the messages, using a rather heavy rubber-tipped stick in each hand for that purpose. The covering of rubber on the ends of the sticks prevents them from splitting the drum and ruining it.

The drum is sometimes housed in a special drum-house for protection from the weather. This house is usually without walls, but it has a good roof of palm fronds to shade the instrument from the blazing sun.

Hollow-log signal slit-drums were quite common in Central America, Colombia, and the Tropical Forest region of South America. They are believed to be possibly of trans-Pacific origin. The panpipes, thought to be also an importation from across the Pacific, were found to be of wider distribution even than the hollow-log slit-drums. The pipes have appeared in all of the different periods of Andean history. Gourd rattles, flutes, jingles (sistrums), and stamping tubes to mark time, were found in considerable number among the aboriginees of Central and South America.

Possibly the most interesting and certainly the most grotesque and fantastic of the slit-drums are those found in Oceana. These are the *priest drums* of the New Hebrides, the Admiralty Islands, New Britain and New Guinea. They may be seen in many of the islands of Oceana, but the best examples are those to be found in the places named.

About seven to twelve feet tall, these creations of primitive imagination are formed to represent beings of wierd character. Beatrice Edgerly's description of the drum groves, in her interesting and informative book, "From the Hunter's Bow," paints a vivid picture: "Near every village of importance a space is cleared to rear the great drum grove. This is the heart and center of all tribal mysteries. Like a mad vision, patchwork of a restless dream, stand the sacred drums, fantastic sentinels upon the danceground.

And here on moonlight nights the natives gather to perform
their special rites. Then the drums take on the appearance
of malevolent monsters, born of neither land nor sea, booming forth in strident tones like angry devils. Daytime shows
them in a less demoniac mood, but no less strange and
startling. Belligerently erect, seven or more feet in height,
they are carved in forms known only to their creators, and
sponsored by their gods.

"Long to be remembered are the black nights resounding
with the ominous voices of the enchanted logs, drumming
out the message that foretells the sacrifice of a new victim
on the morrow, a peace offering to the insatiable gods.

"But then on other nights the drums vibrate victory and
joy. . . . There are occasions when these same monsters
are transformed by some magic spell into the complex character of the native wireless. They then beat out a code
that is caught up and repeated to the farthest corners of
the Island.

"As for the drummer himself, he has at times assumed
the virtuosity of a master, performing rare bits of technical
skill to the delight and amazement of all."*

The voice of the priest drums was thought to be that of
the supernatural. For that reason only the priests of the
tribe were allowed to play them. The drums were made by
expert craftsmen, who created them by hollowing out logs

*Beatrice Edgerly, From the Hunter's Bow.

The Priest Drums of the South Seas represent a high development of the
slit-drum. Resonance and sympathetic resonance gave these fantastic
instruments their good tonal qualities and their imagined supernatural
powers. Primitive man had discovered the hollow sound-chamber and
had built it into his drums.

The Priest Drums of the South Seas.

of very hard resonant wood and then giving them sinister faces and bodies suggested by the savage dictates of primitive imagination. The logs were hollowed until their shells were quite thin, and the large sound-chamber formed in this manner helped to produce a highly sensitive instrument with a clear, almost bell-like tone when struck. Being so thin-walled and sensitive, the hollow priest drums of the drum groves of Oceana would be to a marked degree subject to the phenomenon known as *sympathetic resonance* — that strange power which causes a roaring sound to be heard when one puts a suitable sea shell to his ear, or when he listens to the inside of an empty barrel.

To the savages who created the priest drums, and to the drummers who played them, the drums were gods; for did not the drums speak to them when they put their ears to the longitudinal slit in the drums' hollow bodies and listened? What else could it be but the voice of the god inside the drum?

It was only the drummer-priests who 'understood' the resonant supernatural voices of the priest drums. It was only they who could 'interpret' and execute the never-ending demands of the gods.

The Fish Drum of the Isle of Puto, the Island of Enchantment, the Buddhists' Isle of the Little White Flower. Colorfully lacquered in Chinese red yellow and green, the Fish Drum is a symbol of ceaseless watchfulness, of never closing eyes. Suspended from the ceiling of the temple by U-shaped frames of teakwood, its resonant body is struck by a saffron robed monk to announce the time for prayer and meditation.

would be heard in the tube. This roaring sound manifested in the tube would be that of amplified *inaudible* frequencies with which the resonating chamber is in sympathetic tune. A column of air blown across the opening of the sound chamber would produce the same pitch as that of the roar produced by the inaudible vibrating frequencies which activate its resonance.

If the hollow tube were to be placed to the ear at a time when audible sounds are mingled with the inaudible, both audible and inaudible frequencies will be heard as they are translated into the irregular roar-like tone of the resonating amplifier. If the tube is pressed tightly against the ear, so the molecules of air inside the chamber may not be agitated by external vibrations, silence will result. The roaring will cease, for the activating sympathetic vibrations can not enter the closed chamber and stimulate resonance — unless the vibrations are strong enough to activate the wall of the tube.

A section of bamboo, open at one end, approximately ten inches in length, with an inside diameter of about one inch and three eighths, when struck produces a tone which is roughly E-flat. If the tube is touched ever so lightly a resonance of E-flat will be heard. If its opening is blown across, the sound will be E-flat. If the E-flat just above middle C on the pianoforte is struck, the tube will resonate and amplify this tone quite noticibly. If the tube were to be placed to the ear when no sound is audible, the same tone of E-flat would be heard just the same, on account of its frequencies responding to possibly untold millions of inaudible E-flats which fill the air with their unheard vibrations,

vibrations which are too weak for the unaided human ear to detect.

The flutist who sits calmly in the orchestra with his flute on his lap, his fingers thoughtlessly placed over the holes which would produce a certain note if he were to put the instrument to his lips and blow, can feel his flute vibrate in response to that note when it is played on other nearby instruments of the same register.

Sympathetic resonance and the amplification of inaudible sound were not understood by primitive man. They were as strange and unexplainable to his untutored mind as they still are to our own kindergarten pupils. To him the mysterious roaring sounds he heard in the hollow-bodied drums were not of this world. They were neither the sound of the blood coursing through his head nor the vibrations of actuated and amplified frequencies. They were a message from the supernatural. They were the voice of his god.

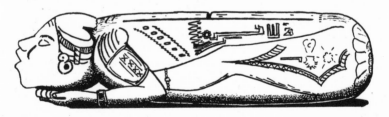

The Mexican slit-drum, or *teponatzli,* is a very ancient instrument of pre-Aztec origin. It is a deep-toned wooden drum developed by the early Mexicans or Mayans into a two-toned instrument of unusual design, the pattern of which has not been found duplicated elsewhere.

Drums have been considered as instruments of melody by

many of their originators. The Chinese, Burmese and most of the peoples of Eastern Asia used drums as melodic expedients, giving each drum a single tone to play; but the ancient Mexicans found a way in which to produce two tones on each of their teponatzlis. This was done by means of a double slit, formed in the shape of a long letter H. The section between the longitudinal slits was cut into two unequal halves, and the two tongues thus formed produced tones of different pitch when struck with the rubber-tipped mallets used in playing them.

The pitch of C-natural is said to have been common to the teponatzlis as a root tone, but with it might be found C-sharp, E-flat, E-natural, F-natural or G-natural as a secondary tone. By combining several instruments, the makers of these ancient two-toned slit-drums used them as melodic vehicles, and the descendants of the original makers claim them to be a primitive xylophone or marimba, rather than a drum.

Teponatzlis have been found carved or decorated with lotus designs,* which shows a common regard for this ancient pattern with Egypt, Oceana, Polynesia and the Far East. One such drum has been found shaped like a monkey, the monkey having ear-plugs, and eyes of gold; but most commonly they are carved with designs of ancient symbols, or formed into shapes resembling pumas, jaguars, alligators or similar animals. Some teponatzlis shaped like humans, or having grotesque human heads, have been found.

*According to certain legends, the lotus blossom was the first flower to appear upon the earth. For that reason it was considered sacred and symbolic of the original motherland — the Garden of Eden.

Many of these instruments, especially those not carved with ancient designs, are thought to have been built after the conquest by Spain, as the conquerors destroyed everything they found related to the civilization they were so determined to eradicate.

In Mexico of today the teponatzli is still used on special occasions. But fortunate is the outsider who is permitted to see one, for they are either safely locked in museums or hidden in secret caves in the remote mountains.

A portable slit-drum made of a single section of bamboo is carried by Malayan watchmen, for use as a signal of alarm. It is an example of the large original instruments, sometimes six or seven feet wide and over twenty feet long, expertly and elaborately carved and played upon by several men, having degenerated into a simple undecorated portable gadget and used in a manner far removed from the originally intended ritualistic purposes.

The *talk-talk* of the Afro-Caribbeans is another example of the slit-drum having become a profane instrument fallen from its ancient esteem, appearance and use.

said to have fallen asleep during his prayers. Upon awakening, he was so ashamed of himself for having dozed, that he immediately cut off his eyelids and tossed them to the roadside so they might never again serve to close his eyes and encourage sleep, and thus offend his god. In the story the eyelids took root and grew into a bush, the leaves of which, when brewed in hot water, make a drink to help those who partake of it to stay awake.

Perhaps the clicking of the priest's temple-block, aided by a bowl of strong hot tea, may now assure him of remaining awake while his prayers are being offered.

A short distance off the coast of southern China, on the Enchanted Island of Puto, the fish-drum *is* shaped like a fish. Its bulging eyes suggest that it has been copied from a member of the goldfish family. Colorfully lacquered in Chinese red, yellow, and blue, the fish drum is a symbol of strength and alertness. Its hollowed form, about eight feet in length, hangs from the ceiling of one of the temples by means of two suspended U-shaped teakwood frames. This wooden fish, which is richly carved in true Oriental manner, is beaten with a club by a saffron robed monk to announce the time for prayer and meditation. The never-closing eyes of the fish are a symbol of vigilance – of ever-wakeful watching.

Unlike the wood-block, which in the orchestra is used singly, or occasionally in pairs, temple-blocks are used in sets consisting of several blocks of different size. The wood-block is seldom called for in standard classical or semi-classical music, but sometimes it is used in lighter works to imitate the click of the claves from which it was developed. Temple-blocks share a similar fate, being used as coloring of equine or an Oriental nature.

Making a wood-block from a single piece of very hard wood requires considerable skill and equipment not available to our first instrument builders, so it is unlikely that primitive man included the slitted wood-block in his first orchestral family.

The earliest form of the slit-drum might easily have been a single section of bamboo with a simple lengthwise slot cut into it, for in the Far East one may still hear the noodle salesman beating his advertising announcement on a small piece of bamboo which seems much too tiny for the far-reaching tone it produces.

WHEN the Early Egyptians learned the art of smelting metals from a more advanced civilization, stone instruments were replaced by those of metal. Many instruments such as cymbals, gongs and bells, formerly made of stone or pottery, were then duplicated or re-styled in the more durable and better-sounding metal. From the small clapper-like castanets and sticks of wood or stone, the triangle was developed. Following the pattern of the xylophone and the marimba, came the orchestra bells, chimes, and the vibraphone. Drums, too, were made of bronze, and instead of the skins wider motion causing all three corners to be struck.

The triangle should be suspended by a thin string, preferably of gut (such as a discarded violin string), so its tone or vibrations will not be dampened in any way.

The high partials or harmonics of the triangle drown its fundamental tone with their metallic dissonances and cause it to produce a very shrill, vibrantly tinkling sound which has no definite pitch. It is a very powerful instrument, and its ability to be heard above the orchestra with but little or no effort on the part of the player has caused the triangle to be called the loudest of all instruments. It should be played very softly, as a usual thing.

The triangle found but little favor with Berlioz, as he felt the occasions in music were so few where it could be used fittingly. "Its metallic noise suits only pieces of an extremely brilliant character when forte, or of a certain wild whimsicality when piano," according to his Treatise on Instruments and Orchestration. When played well, with a delicate touch, it is, however, a most effective addition to the *color* of the orchestra, suggesting the shimmering sparkle of exquisite jewels to the musical score.

The player should provide himself with several triangles of various sizes, starting from a small one measuring about five inches to each side, to others becoming gradually larger until a 'Wagnerian-type' of approximately twelve inches completes his outfit. He should have several pairs of beaters of different thicknesses, weights and degrees of hardness.

The triangle should *never* be struck with a wooden stick, such as a drum stick.

In his First Piano Concerto, the 'Triangle' Concerto, Franz Liszt gave the triangle a very prominent and important part to play. Edvard Grieg made effective use of its delicate vibrancy in Anitra's Dance, from his Peer Gynt Suite. Mozart's Oriental treatment of the triangle and other percussion instruments imitating a Turkish band, in Seraglio (Escape from the Harem), has never been surpassed.

While the triangle has been given an important post in the symphony and opera, it is possible that its most musical charm and satisfying tones may be heard, as they often are, on the farms and ranches of America, where its far-reaching and inviting sounds jangle a welcome call to breakfast, dinner or supper.

In very old music the triangle is sometimes called the 'cymbale,' which is a point to remember whenever the older term is found.

CYMBALS are said to have begun their long and colorful careers as simple pot-covers, and in the musical slang of Elizabethan England they were often called 'clash-pans.' The Chinese originally used two disks of stone for cymbals. These were not struck together, but they were played with wooden mallets instead.

Cymbals of modern design were introduced into the orchestra in 1680, but previous to that time they had been in use for centuries in many parts of the world. Originally there were two distinct types: one kind being worn and played like castanets, using two pairs to produce the proper sound of *antique cymbals,* and another variety requiring but one pair of larger cymbals for striking together; the

An Oriental Version of the Bass Drum and Cymbals.

contact and start the tone by causing the cymbals to vibrate.
If the tone of the cymbals is to be stopped after a beat
has been struck, they are immediately pulled against the
player's chest; but this should not be done so quickly that
the vibrations have not had time to ring for the full value
of the note indicated.

Occasionally the score will call for a *suspended cymbal*
to be played with soft sticks. This timbre is very effective,
as it suggests an atmosphere of mystery or suspense, such
as is created in 'La Mer,' by Claude Debussey, when played softly, or one of tumultuous overpowering sound when
played forte.

It is not good practice to strike the cymbal with a heavy
beater, for not only will the tone be faulty (if a crash is
intended), but a hard straight blow from a heavy beater may
ruin the cymbal as well. A glancing blow is much less
likely to crack a suspended cymbal than one struck straight
down on the instrument.

Often the bass drummer is called upon to play the cymbals, fastening one cymbal to the top of the bass drum and
striking it with another cymbal or beater held in his left
hand. This practice is seldom satisfactory, as the tone and
visual effectiveness of the cymbals cannot be produced in
this manner. "This economical proceeding is intolerable,"
says Berlioz, "the cymbals, losing their sonority, produce
a noise which might be compared to the fall of a sack of
ironmongery and broken glass. It has a trivial character, de-
prived of all pomp and brilliancy, and is fit for nothing
better than to make dance-music for monkeys, or to accompany the feats of jugglers, mountebanks and swallowers of

cultured American races, previous to their conquest. The form best known is the hawk-bell, or common sleigh-bell of the North. The globular body is suspended by a loop at the top and is slit on the underside, so that the tinkling of the small, free pellets of metal may be audible." It is thought that such bells may have originated in Mexico and Central America. Dr. Holmes continues: "There is strong evidence that such bells were used by the Americans before the advent of the whites. . . . The American origin of the bells, therefore, is not to be questioned. The form originated, no doubt, in a rattle, at first a nutshell or a gourd, later modeled in clay, and in time worked out in metal."

The Chinese, too, lay claim to the invention of the bell; but having invented it, they could devise no way in which to suspend it, until the sight of monkeys hanging by their tails gave them the idea for the little extra loop at the top for that purpose.

Bells were not originally intended to call the congregation to church, as they now are, but they were rung to frighten evil spirits away from places of worship. In this respect bells are related to the sistrum and the rattle, for the earliest function of the prototype of these instruments may well have been that of frightening the ancient bogeyman and goblins away from our contemporary infants' primitive counterparts.

Bells of many shapes and sizes have been made by widely separated peoples. These range in magnitude from the tiny cherry-shaped bells worn on pussy's neck, to the larger ones adorning the Sheik's camel, the Rajah's favorite elephant, Mrs. Clancy's cow, and those still larger to be found in our schools and churches. The famous Liberty Bell of America is a fine example of a large bell; but the big bell of Peking, China — which was rung only when the Emperor prayed for rain — weighs fifty-three tons, or 118,720 pounds. It was cast in the 15th century. By comparison, 'Big Ben' of London is not very large, as it weighs only thirteen and one-half tons. The world's largest bell, known as the 'Czar's Bell,' in Moscow, weighs 433,722 pounds!

A primitive bell of teakwood is used as a curfew in some Buddhist monasteries. The bell, which is struck with a wooden mallet, is approximately three inches thick and it is shaped into a rectangle about twelve by fourteen inches. The two upper corners are mitred so the top half of this flat wooden bell has the appearance of one-half of an eight-sided figure. A hole is bored in the upper section and a cord is looped through it, so the bell may be held by the saffron-robed monk who strikes it to announce the time to retire and to cease all noise and conversation.

Teakwood is a favorite material for making bells in the Far East. Bells for the ubiquitous caraboa, or water buffalo, are made with a wooden clapper inside the bell. Some large elephant bells of the same wood have two clappers hung on the outside of the bell form.

An unusual kind of wooden bell is to be found on Taiwan. (Formosa) Poles of about six feet in length have attached to their ends heavier pieces of wood which resemble crude culinary implements. These end pieces vary in length from approximately one to two feet, and they are about six inches in diameter. Each 'bell' has a different sound when it is dropped or pounded on the large flat stone which is used meaning 'bells,' and 'spiel' meaning 'play.'

There are several compositions in which the orchestra bells have an important part. As these are difficult, the player should familiarize himself with them before trying to play them in an orchestra. 'Forest Murmurs,' (or 'Waldweben,') by Richard Wagner, is one of the pieces the player should know almost by memory, if he is to play it well with the woodwinds of the orchestra. The 'Sorcerer's Apprentice,' by Paul Dukas, is another. The 'Bell Song' from Delibes' opera, 'Lakme,' and the 'Violin Concerto,' and 'Marionettes' from 'Raymonda Ballet,' by Glazounow, have bell parts not easily played at sight.

The noisy cowbells used in the Latin music of rhumba bands are reminiscent of the ancient stone and ceramic bells, such as those used by the first musicians; but the only people to retain and still use primitive instruments of stone are the Polynesians, who use the ili-ili and the po-ha-ku in their native dances, and the Chinese and the Koreans, who use the *pien-king* in their Royal Orchestra.

The pien-king is a quaint instrument consisting of sixteen heavy stones graduated in size, each shaped like a carpenter's square. The stones are suspended from a highly decorated rack, back of which sits the player who strikes them with a wooden mallet. The chimes have a delicate bell-like sound, which is of a sweet, musical nature.

Chinese theorists consider the sound of stone as one of the most beautiful of all timbres, claiming that it has a brighter sound than that of wood, and a less tart and rasping one than metal. It is thought by them also to have more brilliance and a sweeter tone than either wood or metal.

The *tse-king*, or 'sonorous stone,' is another of the ancient Chinese bells. It is made of a marble-like agate which contains a small amount of iron. One of these old stone instruments of Chinese origin has been discovered in the ruins left by an unknown archaic race in Peru,* thus indicating that there must have been commerce and communication between Asia and the Americas long before the present civilization. This possibility is further suggested by the fact that the shepherds' pipes (the syrinx of the Greeks) of the 'Incas' of today have the five-toned scale of the Chinese, and pipes of this same description have been found encased with pre-Inca mummies of remote antiquity. The remains of a canal for boats to pass through has been discovered atop the Andes. This canal must date back to a time when there were no mountains on the American continents, and the Amazon basin was a large sea.

Significant pictures on the pottery left by this ancient Andean race shows them to have had almond-shaped eyes, and to have worn sandals similar to those of the Japanese of today. Their successors include seaweed in their diets, as is now the custom in the Far East. They had similar musical instruments!

"The great Mayas . . . The Toltecs . . . The Aztecs," writes Beatrice Edgerly, in 'From the Hunter's Bow,' "Their origins remain a problem for the archaeologists. From where did they come? Which seas and mountains witnessed their migrations? Oddly enough, convincing proof points to the East. Music adds its own argument to

*Col. James Churchward, The Children of Mu.

their oriental beginnings, and like the Incas, their harmonies moved on the pentatonic scale of the Chinese."

The golden spangled walls of Cuzco must have appeared quite similar to the conquistadores in Peru to those seen by Marco Polo when he visited Cathay and Zipangu.*

*China and Japan.

Rattle Rapture.

CHAPTER III

Rattles and Gourds

AN INSTRUMENT of almost equal antiquity and importance to the claves in primitive ritual and music is the *rattle*. We may feel certain of this if for no other reason than that it is the instrument which follows in natural order to an infant after he has demonstrated an interest in the claves or their contemporary equivalent. The rattle is the first real musical instrument a child is likely to possess.

At the beginning of the nineteenth century the Drum was the only object of worship on almost the entire South American continent. This fetish was not limited to South America alone, but it extended from the Strait of Magellan to the Arctic Circle, skipping only Yucatan and Mexico, where more ancient civilizations flourished and where different gods and religions prevailed. It covered an area embracing all of Northern Siberia, Greenland and Lapland, and continued in an almost unbroken sequence to the southernmost tip of Patagonia, Tierra del Fuego.

The drum worshipped in this vast expanse was not the drum with heads of skin. It was the rattle-drum, the *maraca*.

The first rattle-drums were simply dried gourds in which their own seeds provided the sounding agent. Small pebbles were added eventually, to increase the sound; but, according to the primitive mind, in order to be potent, a rattle-drum must contain seeds of some kind to provide the necessary magic for the ritual in which it is used. Indian corn, wheat, wild rice, dried peas, sometimes dried beans were used; but the maraca demanded seeds of some variety or other, for seeds have within them that mysterious spark of life which puts the primitive mind in direct touch with the supernatural, the unknowable. The pebbles, bits of shell, or even buck-shot helped the sound of the rattle-drum, but seeds gave it magic potency.

The American Indians carried the idea of the rattle to the sticks with which they beat their tom-toms. The heads of the beaters were coiled into a circular end and then covered with skin into which were placed seeds and small stones. The rattle of the sticks made an interesting sound as it combined with that of the drum, and the magic powers of the medicine-man using this dual drum were two-fold.

A modern version of the primitive stick-rattle may now be found in the hollow shot-filled felt-covered tympani sticks, which may be used on either kettledrums or tom-toms.

Lapland and Brazil were the seats of rattle-worship. The mystic powers of the rattle made possible all the magic of the Lapland sorcerer. With its aid he was able to divine the wishes of his gods and learn what sacrifices they desired. His drum established a communication for him with the spirits. With it he could predict the future. To the Brazilians the maraca was the dwelling-place of their devil, so they offered sacrifices to the drum itself.

The religion involving the worship of the rattle, or drum, was so thoroughly a part of the habits of the people of such an immense domain, so similar in aspect was it that it would seem to warrant the conclusion that at some time in the distant past the cult of drum-worship might have been a universal one.

Today at shrines in Korea, one may see a chanting priest who carries a gourd rattle in his left hand. As he recites his prayer, the priest gently taps the rattle with a stick to attract and hold his god's attention.*

The rattle seems to have been presented to primitive man in much the same mysterious manner that the claves were. Our early ancestors merely found a seed-filled dried gourd and discovered that it had an interesting sound when it was shaken. Experiments disclosed that harder seeds placed inside the shell of a dried gourd or cocoanut improved the sound and made it more resonant. It was learned that beads loosely strung and fitted around the outside of a large plump gourd also made a very good rattle.

The manner in which Nature placed a seed-filled gourd or any other form of rattle instrument in the hands of ancient man was no more understandable to him than it is at present to our infants, when they are presented with a rattle of rubber or plastic from the nearby dime-store, with one made of skin if the child is a native of the frozen North, or with a home-made wooden one if he happens to be born in the Far East.

*In a similar manner the jingles of the Salvation Army tambourines sound when a coin is dropped on their inverted heads. They, too, call attention to the fact that the doner is contributing "for Jesus' sake."

THE GOURD family of vegetables has served man in various capacities throughout the ages. As food it includes the watermelons, squashes, pumpkins and cucumbers. Many gourds are used for ornaments, both in the growing state and after having been dried. The towel gourd is used, as its name implies, for dishcloths or bath sponges. Very young fruits of this variety are edible. Other gourds are used as containers for water, as they keep the liquid cool even in warm weather. The bottle gourd has been called the original thermos bottle. Some gourds are used as nest-eggs, so nearly do they look like eggs. Others may attain fabulous sizes, as diameters of two feet and lengths of three are not uncommon in some parts of the world. Pipes for smoking and dippers for water have long been made from gourds. Before the invention of paper- or metal-cased cartridges for guns, powder horns were sometimes made from gourds that Nature seems to have designed especially for that very purpose. Gourds not only have served as toys for children, but the growing of gourds has continued to be a delightful way of encouraging children to have an interest in plants.

The gourd has been one of the most generous contributors to the development of music, too. Gourds have served as rattles, or *maracas*, so important to primitive music, magic and ritual. They have served as scratchers, or *guiros*, as resonators for the xylophone and marimba, and as windchests for primitive pipe organs. They are still used occasionally as mutes for French horns and trombones.

A unique drum has survived from the ancient races of Mexico, and it is still in use by the primitive people to be found in the less modernized sections of that interesting land. This instrument, which is considered to be indigenous to Mexico, consists of a section of a large gourd which is inverted and floated in an ample container of water. When this gourd-drum is beaten with a stick it delivers an amazing amount of tone and carrying power.

One of the most unusual uses for the gourd is to be found in China and Korea. An ancient instrument, not of the rattle type, but one so old that its origin dates back to mythical ages, is the Chinese mouth-organ, or *cheng*. The body of this primitive pipe-organ is a gourd, into which is fitted a wooden mouthpiece and seventeen bamboo pipes of various lengths, each having small tongues of metal attached to their lower ends by means of beeswax. The vibrations of of the little reeds of metal produce the tones of this ancient instrument, while the gourd serves as a wind-chest.

The cheng is claimed to be the most perfect of Chinese instruments, both in sweetness of tone and in delicacy of construction. The principle used in combining the gourd and bamboo pipes is that of our grand organ. Its introduction into Europe led to the invention of the bagpipe, the accordion, harmonica, and the harmonium.*

Another strange instrument made of a plump gourd and three sticks is used by the natives of Panama. A large gourd is first relieved of its seeds and pulp, and then it is

*An instrument which is a missing link between the *cheng* and the modern pipe organ may be seen in Las Pinas Church, not far from the city of Manila, in the Philippine Islands. This unique organ has 950 pipes made of bamboo, but the original bellows for filling the wind-chest was replaced in 1932 with an electric blower. The construction of the organ began in 1818, by Father Diego Cera.

pierced with properly placed holes to accommodate three strong slender branches that are fitted through them. After the branches are installed through the gourd they are bent into a bow, and their ends are fitted with taut vines for strings. The gourd with its three bows is raised in the air on a pole about fifteen feet long, and the wind which sings through this primitive aeolian harp causes it to hum cheerfully with the slightest breeze. The gourd serves as a resonator, and amplifies the sound caused by the wind.

Besides being a perfect rattle for primitive man, both past and present, the gourd with its natural resonating body provides the material for an improved notched stick, the *guiro*. After drying, a long cucumber-shaped gourd is emptied of its seeds and pulp through a square or rectangular hole cut in its back, and a mouth-like opening at the larger end. V-shaped notches are then cut across the the top of the central section of its body. A design of some sort is drawn, painted or carved at either or both ends of the instrument thus created, and it is ready to be played upon by having a stiff scraper of bone, hard wood, or a thin metal rod drawn briskly over the notches, as it is held by the hole which was cut in its back for removing the seeds and pulp.

Nature placed another rattle instrument in the hands of ancient man in addition to the gourd and the cocoanut. This rather gruesome specimen was made of the dried jawbone of an ass or zebra, in which the teeth still in their sockets, though loosened by age and exposure, would produce delightful buzzing sounds when the instrument was struck or shaken. It also made an excellent scraping drum when a hard stick or similar object was rubbed across the teeth.

Like other primitive musical instruments which were used also as missiles and weapons, the jawbone rattle-scraper served in this double capacity. Its use as a weapon is recorded in Chapter XV, 15th verse of Judges, in the Old Testament of the Bible, for therein is stated: "And he (Sampson) found a new jawbone of an ass, and put forth his hand, and took it, and slew a thousand men therewith."

Primitive man seems to have been not too fastidious in his selection of toys or instruments, but the unlovely jaw-bone rattle has withstood the test of time and public opinion, for it is still in use today.

The bamboo-rattle, or *pu-ili* of the Polynesians, is a variation of the gourd rattle, although it bears more resemblance to a clapper than it does to a rattle. The pu-ili is made by shredding a section of bamboo into a broom-like instrument to be struck against the player's arm or shoulder, against its mate held in the player's other hand, or swished on the side of a drum. The bamboo rattle is still used in the Polynesian South Seas to join the hula orchestras in accompanying gay songs and dances. This instrument of bamboo is sometimes asked for in symphonic music of European origin, too, such as that of Richard Strauss or Gustav Mahler. It is then called the *ruthe,* and is beaten or swished on the shell of the bass drum.

The Yuma Indians use round willow sticks about an inch in diameter and about a foot long, two being held in the player's right hand and used together, never singly. These stick rattles are used with certain classes of songs, while with others the singer uses two bundles of arrowweed, eighteen or more inches in length and about an inch and one-half in thickness at the place where the sticks are tied together.

Neither the maraca nor the guiro have much asked of them in most of the music we now hear, excepting the Latin-American rhumba type, in which they have a place of importance. The sharp rattle of the maracas, however, may have furnished the desire-pattern which led to the snare drum. The swishy smoothness of the gourd rattle's gentler moods is often imitated with wire brushes played on the snare drum, or with sandpaper-blocks, in our music of popular style.

Sandpaper-blocks may easily be made by first selecting two pieces of soft wood measuring about three and one-half or four inches wide, eight or nine inches long, by three-quarters of an inch thick; then gluing similarly sized pieces of one-fourth or three-eighths inch medium-soft felt on the least attractive side of each block. After the glue is dry a piece of medium grade flint- or garnet-paper is fastened over the felt and far enough up the sides of the wood to allow the paper to be held in place with thumb-tacks. The purpose of the felt is to prevent a clapping noise when the two blocks are rubbed together — so the result will be an all sandpaper sound, instead of one marred by percussive knocks.

The 'Mosquito Dance,' by Paul White, is an interesting example of the use of sandpaper-blocks in the orchestra. A timely slap-stick solo at the end of the piece brings it to a meaningful happy ending.

LONG before our early instrument makers had acquired the knowledge and craftsmanship needed to manufacture cymbals, gongs and bells of metal, they had created an instrument so fascinating and so widely popular that it not only influenced the invention of some of our modern instruments of percussion, but it has itself remained in use in certain parts of the world during countless centuries of time. This instrument, a relative of the seed-filled gourd rattle, is the *sistrum*.

The dictionary tells us that a sistrum is "an instrument consisting of a thin metal frame, through which is passed a number of metal rods, and furnished with a handle by which it is shaken and made to jingle." It tells further that the sistrum was peculiar to the Egyptians, who used it in the worship of Isis and to frighten away evil spirits.

Previous to the time the Egyptians used the sistrum in their ritual of worship, or to scare evil spirits from their temples, it had been developed through a vast period of time until the original forked stick with a few shells on it to shake and rattle became the instrument of metal found with the Egyptians of the Old or Middle Kingdoms.

Sistrums of somewhat the original form may be seen today in use by the fishermen of Malaya and Melanesia. The form of this device resembles the shape of a two-pronged fork or a tennis racket. The framework is made of rattan. Fitted in between the arms of the fork is a crossbar on which are strung several cocoanut shells, or the shells may be strung on the frame itself. Some say this ancient rattle is used to attract sharks while fishing. Others claim it is used to frighten them away. Eskimos use a similar rattle to entice seals into the water.

From a beginning in a no longer existing land south and east of southern Asia, a forgotten land with but its countless ancient mountain tops now standing above the endless island-dotted sea, the sistrum traveled to many parts of the world. East to the Americas, where the early settlers found a place for it in their scheme of life, and whose retrograde descendants, the Yaqui of Mexico and the Kadiuveo of South America, still retain its use; while Hopi priests of our own great Southwest use a special sistrum, the *pa-a-ya*, which consists of jingling shells, gourds and grasses held on a long crooked stick. It traveled west to Ancient Egypt, to Greece and Mesopotamia, where sistrums similar to those of the Yaqui and the Kadiuveo have been discovered.

While on its long journey throughout the world the sistrum was re-styled from its crude original design, for during that period of its existence the Age of Metal was ushered in, and such an important and magically potent implement as the sistrum was bound to be made of brass, bronze, silver or iron, instead of the lesser materials of more primitive peoples. During the Old and Middle Kingdoms of Egypt, the sistrum became a horseshoe-like frame with a handle, having a few thin metal rods loosely fixed across it. Upon the rods were strung several small cymbal-like disks which jingled when the instrument was shaken.

The sistrum was known as 'Mohammed's Standard' in Arabia, where it became very popular. When it traveled to Turkey it was called the 'Crescent' — "an upright pole decorated with a fanciful half-Oriental headpiece of metal, composed of a crescent and other symbols, from which bells, jingles . . . were suspended.''*

The crescent found its way into Turkey from Central Asia or China, where it was used by the orchestra leader to give the signal for the music to start playing. In the form of the drum major's baton, or the conductor's 'stick,' descendants of the ancient sistrum still perform similar functions in the music of today, although they have degenerated into instruments to be *seen,* but not heard.

The word 'sistrum' is derived from the Greek 'sistron,' meaning 'thing shaken,' so actually the sistrum is a special kind of rattle. The little jingles incorporated into its design, however, have been carried on to an instrument with which we are more familiar: the *tambourine.*

*Curt Sachs, The History of Musical Instruments.

The Sistrum.

In the colder parts of the world gourds could not be grown, so — that he might satisfy his inborn desire for a friction instrument to scratch on — primitive man living outside of the gourd belt hit upon the idea of cutting notches in a stick and then rubbing another stick rapidly over them in order to produce the fascinating tonal effect the Creator had implanted in his mind. But he found that a plain notched stick lacked resonance, no matter how fancifully he carved it with grotesque designs or painted it with bizarre heads and faces. It was not a satisfactory instrument upon which to scrape and play.

Probably it took many, many long years, but eventually some clever man-animal discovered that more resonance could be produced and a louder tone brought forth from his *morache*, if a hollow bowl-shaped dish, a tightly woven basket, or a tortoise shell were placed under it. With the sound-chamber provided by a large shell, a pottery dish, or in later years a tin can, the notched stick became an acceptable resonant instrument.

An early example of the morache was carved of wood in the shape of a crouching tiger on whose back were cut twenty-seven saw-like teeth. In use, the head of the tiger was struck three times with a piece of split bamboo, which was then rubbed briskly over the serrations on its back. A similar instrument was used in Japan. The Indians of the Amazon used bamboo for their moraches. The primitive Javanese carved wooden birds with deep notches on their backs. Some North American Indians used a stick shaped like the jawbone of a bear; the notches were cut to resemble the bear's teeth, and the bone of a bear was used as the rubbing device. The instrument was used in a ceremonial Bear Dance, and the sound produced represented the growling of the bear. Yaqui Indians made scraping sticks from dried ribs of the sahauro cactus. They were about two feet long, cut with shallow notches over which was rubbed a slender stick of greasewood.

While the ancient Mexicans used gourds for their scratching instruments, they also made special ones from human bones and from the shells of tortoises: *ayotls*. It is interesting to note that the Aztec word 'ayotl' has the double meaning of 'turtle' and 'gourd.' The same may be said of the word 'coc' in the language of the natives of Guatamala.

In the almost obliterated civilization of an antedated Mexico, a unique form of the morache was devised. This ancient scratching instrument was called the *tzicahuaztli*, or the *omitzicahuaztli*. It was made from the thigh bone of a deceased friend or foe.

Scratching instruments of this kind were used by the Aztecs during funeral ceremonies or celebrations for captives sacrificed after battles, or for services in honor of fallen comrades. The bone was crossed by fifteen deeply cut notches, over which was scraped another hard object, such as a bone or a piece of horn. The speed of the scraping action was varied in order to raise or lower the pitch of the sound produced, in a manner quite like that of the small boy who runs his thumb nail over the teeth of a comb.

El Morache precortesiano. An inverted basket serves as the resonator for this primitive scraping-stick. Gourds were sometimes used. Sometimes tortoise shells, or tin cans. Without a sound chamber, the notched stick was not a satisfactory musical instrument.

El morache precortesiano.

The music played on the bone guiro was "very sad and doleful," according to the brave conquistadores.

While of wide distribution, the notched stick (morache or guayos) seems to have been used only in the Western Hemisphere. North Americans from Alaska to Mexico made and used this instrument, as well as a hollowed split stick. The split stick is a castanet-like clapper, which the Indians of the North decorated with carved designs of their tribe, or family totems.

The guiro (scraper, morache or guayos) has not been given a place in the modern orchestra in its own physical form, excepting in Latin-type music. It has, however, played a very important part in the development of an entire group of musical instruments: the instruments which are played by means of friction—the bow-played instruments, in other words; for whoever draws a bow across the strings of a violin, viola, 'cello, or a stringbass, is actually playing a descendant of the guiro, just as surely as is the boy who scrapes a stick along a picket fence, or who places a piece of paper or cardboard in the spokes of his bicycle in order to produce the particular sound that primitive man learned to make on a notched dried gourd, a notched section of bamboo with one end open, or on a hardwood stick with a serrated edge.

CHAPTER IV

Tom-toms

LEGENDS tell of times before there were mountains upon the face of Earth, and of times before our planet had a moon; but to actually and specifically penetrate the veil of obscurity which hides the early history of man and his musical instruments and then name a definite date or even an era during which our most ancient instruments took form and developed, would indeed be quite impossible. No matter how far back we go into history or pre-history, however, we can find no evidence of man's existence when he did not have musical instruments of some sort.

On account of the many ages since passed and the great geological and geographic changes in our earth's surface during past ages, the earliest proofs of human habitation are dissipated and obliterated beyond the possibility of recognition or reconstruction, except through comparison with environmental circumstances surrounding primitive people still living under Stone Age conditions.

Certain tribes of south central Asia reckon their years beginning from the time the Himalayas were raised. Chinese records date back 40,000 years. In west central Texas stone implements thought to be 70,000 years old have been discovered under thirty feet of dirt. Science sets 750,000 years as the period elapsed since primitive man left the first recognizable traces of his existence. A recent discovery in an Italian coal mine names eleven million years as the age of the human skeleton found embedded far below the surface. Only 10,000 years have passed since our earliest settlers lived on the shores of the now dry Lake Cochise in southeastern Arizona; but through the blood-type of their descendants, the American Indians, a relationship has been established between them and the natives of the Philippine Islands and with the Eskimos of the north polar regions.*

Originally, some 150,000,000 years ago, the Araucarian trees of Arizona's Petrified Forests grew at an elevation of approximately one mile; but changes in the structure of the earth's surface caused the whole area to sink and become a sea. The trees were lowered to a depth of 3000 feet, where, beneath the sea, chemical action changed the wood of the trees into agate. A later shift in the crust raised them again to an elevation of 5000 feet above sea level, at which height they may now be seen.

The Salton Sea of Southern California is at present 265 feet *below* sea-level, while on the top of nearby lofty mountains coral reefs give mute evidence of the past. The sands and shells of an ancient beach rest at the foot of these high mountains, proclaiming an intermediate period. The remains of certain corals which can live only at ocean depths no greater than one-hundred feet have recently been dredged from depths of a mile or more in the Pacific, and sand and pebbles from ancient *seashore beaches* have been gotten lately from great depths in the mid-Atlantic.**

These and other easily substantiated facts give positive
*McNickle, They Came Here First.   **National Geographic Magazine.

proof of marked changes in the earth's geographical structure in times gone by. They provide a logical reason for the great migrations of past eras, and for the distribution and similarity of drums and implements over the entire world. They give as well a reason for extremely ancient musical instruments ·not having been easily found and recognized.

The first Americans were not native of this continent, for the remains of, or even the slightest trace of an anthropoid stock from which they might have evolved has never been discovered. Unfortunately, the musical life of our earliest immigrants cannot be known except through what is shown in the music of their descendants and in the evolutionary traits of our human young. It is of interest, however, to note that in a later prehistoric period the cavemen of Southern France left concrete evidence of musical development through the two bone whistles or flutes found among their relics.

"In an ancient dolman, or sepulchre near Poictiers was found a partly complete flute made of stag's horn. The distance of the holes, and shape of the mouthpiece, show an aptitude of construction and an experience in acoustics. . . . Another instrument is more interesting yet," continues Louis C. Elston, in The Curiosities of Music. "It was discovered by M. Lartet in a ravine, along with bones of animals now extinct in France. It is a flute (straight and with a mouthpiece), with finger holes. It is made of the bone of a reindeer, which seems a proof positive of its being made at a time when the climate and zoology of France were totally different from the present."

The American Indian and His Drum.

The fact that flutes or whistles, rather than rattles or drums were discovered, shows that caveman musical culture had advanced far beyond the primary stages. This observation is further borne out by the high artistic quality of the drawings, etchings, painting and sculpture found in the caves.

Legends of the North American Indians tell of the Drum as far back as the last Deluge. The Chinese tanned pig-skins for use as drumheads for over thirty-five centuries before Christ, but nevertheless they were not the inventors of the drum with heads of skin. Drums of this type, which are called *tom-toms,* are said to have been introduced into China from the enigmatic and dramatic Gobi Desert region of Central Asia.

The urge to create drums of this kind seems to have been a universal one, for tom-toms of various degrees of crudeness have been discovered among all primitive peoples. But few aboriginees have been found who were so under-developed culturally that they did not use this instrument some way in their scheme of everyday life.

The American Indian and His Drum. A skin stretched over a form of some kind is a comparatively recent development of the drum. Add a few seeds to its beater and it is a rattle-drum. Fasten some jingles to it and the tom-tom is a tambourine. Stretch some strings across its head and it is a snare drum. Expand its size and it becomes a bass drum. Shape it like a bowl, and provide it with a means for tuning its head, and it is a kettledrum!

IT WAS A GLORIOUS day in the annals of percussion instruments when one of our ancestors discovered, probably quite by accident, the wonderful resonant sound that is produced when a tightly stretched skin is struck.

The first of our forebears to notice its unusual resonance and its strange response to the mysterious phenomenon of *sympathetic vibration,* imagined the drum consisting of a skin stretched between poles or stakes, or at one end of a hollow log or stump, to be a god — or perhaps the voice of a great spirit. It was supernatural.

Almost everyone has felt an unmistakable vibration in something being carried in his hands or under his arm when passing near a running automobile, a train, or in fact anything making a noise. A book or other sensitive object held in the hand seems to quiver or vibrate if a bus or streetcar goes by, or if a loud whistle is blown. Large heavy glass doors and windows have been broken by the *sound* of sirens or explosions. A properly pitched note played on a violin may shatter a drinking glass to bits.

Both music and noise are composed of sound. Music being a pleasant sound, usually associated with rhythm; while noise is unpleasant, unmusical, and usually lacking in rhythm. Both music and noise are caused by vibrations, sound waves.

A musical tone, set in motion by whatever means prescribed for the instrument of its origin, consists of vibra-

A Stretched Skin as a Drum. It is highly probable that the first drums consisted of only a skin stretched between poles or stakes, or even stretched by the players themselves, as they pulled tightly with one hand while they beat the skin with a club held in the other.

A Stretched Skin as a Drum.

tions of certain frequencies, which for their pitch (high or low) depend upon the size and structure of the musical unit being played. The sound waves, or vibrations, set in motion on one instrument, or object, have an affinity for vibrations of the same frequency embodied in other nearby objects or instruments, and the energy created by the vibrations of one may be transmitted through the air to another object or instrument having the same frequency.

If two tuning forks of similar pitch were held or mounted in an upright position and placed even several yards apart, then one of the two struck in order to have its vibrations motivated and its tone heard, the other fork would vibrate and respond with audible sound. The vibrations of the fork sounding through being in 'sympathy' with the frequency of the other will continue sounding after the vibrations of the fork originally struck have been stopped and silenced.

This phenomenon, the opposite of tonal annulment, is known as *sympathetic vibration*. It is characteristic not only of music, but it may be caused by any sound finding similar frequencies to vibrate in whatever may be within range of its influence. The reverberations of rumbling thunder, the roaring of the angry surf, or even the vibrations set in motion by the sound of a human voice would cause primitive man's drum to react physically, so the vibrations could be·*felt* on its skin, or to react audibly, so its response to the laws of physics could be *heard*.

When our first drummers talked near their drum, or perhaps to it, the drum seemed to answer them, as it reacted to the then unknown laws of sympathetic vibration; so it is no wonder that the drum was worshipped as a god in so many parts of the primitive world.

The tightly stretched skin forming the head of a drum gave it resonance and great sensitivity. This fascinating quality led our earliest drum-makers to explore the possibilities of their newly found instrument, and to build many types of drums with heads of skin.

At first these early builders were concerned chiefly with trying different kinds of skins for the heads of their instruments and with making the shells, or bodies of the drums, in different shapes. Some drums were fashioned quite flat and hoop-like, with only one head stretched over it. Others had barrel-shaped bodies, with a head at one end or both. Small-sized drums were found to have a higher pitched tone than did the larger ones. Using them in pairs, a small drum and a larger one – a higher tone and a lower one – proved very fascinating to hear and to play. Such pairs eventually became our *bongo* drums.

The two small joined 'bongo' drums of the modern rhumba band have their origin with the African Bongo tribe. In common with all Negro races, the Bongos are enthusiastic lovers of music. Originally their kettle-shaped drums were made from the thick trunk of a tamarind tree, a section of which was hollowed into cylindrical form with one end larger than the other. Both ends were then covered with goat skin, from which the hair was removed. At nightly ceremonies (or orgies) the Bongos kept bright fires burning in order to prevent their drums from becoming damp and dull-toned in the moist tropical atmosphere of Equatorial Africa.

The original giant Bongo drums, formerly beaten with

heavy clubs by powerful blows, have since degenerated, or progressed, into perhaps more interesting rhythmic instruments which are held between the player's knees as he taps them with his fingers.

A skin stretched over a bowl-shaped dish or kettle produces a tone of more resonance and musical quality than it does otherwise. Drums of this kind were made in a great many sizes, and many different materials were used to form the bowl-shaped resonators which reflect the sounds and improve their quality. Eventually they became known as *kettledrums,* on account of the kettle-like shape of their 'bowls,' or bodies; and so popular were the kettledrums and so musical their tone, that means were devised whereby they could be tuned to a definite pitch.

The kettledrums have been given a place of great prominence and importance in the modern symphony orchestra. Their development from crude bowl-shaped tom-toms to the most fascinating instrument of all will be disclosed in subsequent chapters.

The desire to create tom-toms, or *drum-drums*, as we might have called them in those days long gone by, seems to have been prevalent the world over. And primitive man built them from whatever available material there was: wood, bone, pottery or metal — metal in the form of tin cans, after civilization invaded the homes of still uncultured people. But long before this recent event occurred, copper provided a most suitable material for use in the construction of drums and other articles.

Sometimes these early drums appeared with but one head. Sometimes with two — and sometimes with none at all, as was the case with the *pandorella,* which is a tambourine having jingles, but no head! The pandorella of rural Spain has its opposite in the large tambourine-shaped tom-tom of Russia; which consists of a narrow shell, over which is stretched a head — but instead of being beaten like a tom-tom, this drum is played with the fingers and hands, tambourine fashion. It has no jingles.

The tom-tom has been found as a huge hollowed log with a skin stretched at one end, or at both. Again it was a skin stretched over a hoop of bone or wood, to be held by a handle in one hand and struck on its rim with a beater held in the other. Chinese tom-toms differ from all others, for they have large-headed nails of crude design for fastening the thick pigskin heads to the body of the drum; and those traditionally correct are made of either cedar, mulberry or sandalwood.

Travelers of the final decades of the nineteenth century tell of the tom-tom being the only instrument of the Eskimos living along the north coast of Alaska. The drum of these

Eskimo Drummers.

primitive people consisted of merely a circle of wood or baleen (whalebone) from twelve to eighteen inches in diameter, over which a tightly stretched skin was fastened by means of braided sinews. The bladder of a whale was sometimes used for this purpose, but the preferred skin was that of a whale's tongue. The instrument had a handle attached for holding it in the left hand while the player beat on the back of the hoop with a stick. Drums of similar character were found among all of the northern people, especially the Laps and Greenlanders.

The great tribe of Sioux Indians used three distinct types of tom-toms, each for a different purpose; and not a single tribe of Indians who lacked a great esteem and respect for the drum in their tribal and personal customs has ever been found. The tom-tom was of divine origin, according to their beliefs, and it was given many offices to perform. It not only served to conjure the spirits of the departed, it frightened them away as well. It served to tell the Indian maiden of a declaration of love, or the enemy of a declaration of war. The effects of atmospheric conditions on its head or heads made the drum an excellent prophet for short range predicting of approaching storms.

The heads of drums are greatly influenced by atmospheric conditions. When the air is clear and dry, owing to a high-

Eskimo Drummers. The tightly stretched walrus hide covering of the Eskimo's kayak makes a very resonant drum. It may be played with flat sticks or paddles. The hoop-drum, which usually consists of the skin of a whale's tongue stretched over a narrow frame, is beaten with a short club similar to the 'knockers' used to dispatch salmon or seals. Eskimo 'musicals' are sometimes held inside the snow igloos. Men play the drums, but the women are allowed only to chant.

pressure area, they become tight and the tone will be high-pitched and brilliant; but when a low-pressure area brings dampness, the drumheads will stretch (loosen) and sound with a dull, low-pitched tone.

Primitive man began to associate the sound of his drum with the condition of the weather. He found that he could rely on his drum as a weather-prophet! Its being either high or low in pitch kept him advised as to what sort of weather he might expect in the immediate future.

When considering primitive man's educational background and his lack of understanding relative to the physical properties of hides or skins, as they react to vibrations and to the weather, it is easily understandable that he might have been filled with awe, fear and respect at their seeming supernatural attributes — their 'god-like' qualities.

The Huehuetl.

Single-headed tom-toms of archaic design sometimes were so long that they had to be suspended from trees or from roofs in order to be played upon. The lengths of these tubular drums were in time shortened so they could be played in a vertical position. The open bottoms of the shortened drums were imbedded in dirt or sand, and that this might more easily be accomplished, their lower ends were cut into three or four tooth-like shapes. These are the *footed drums*. When the ground was hard, instead of loose or sandy, the footed drums were placed on stands of appropriate patterns, or allowed to rest directly on the floor while being played.

Footed drums are to be found in Oceana, Polynesia, Africa and the West Indies; but the most elaborate and unusual ones were a product of ancient Mexico.

The primitive footed drum of prehistoric Mexico is the *huehuetl*. Its very name, 'old-old,' tells of its great age. The huehuetl was a drum of war and sacrifice. Carved artistically and significantly with symbols of Battle, Fire, and the Sun, it was a sacred instrument of a former civilization in Mexico.

The skin of a cougar or jaguar was fastened over one end of this drum, which was made in a variety of styles ranging up to three or four feet in height and as big around as a man's body. Means were provided in the huehuetl so its pitch could be raised or lowered to match that of the sing-

The Huehuetl. The 'old-old' drum of ancient Mexico was tuned by means of tourniquets, one of the earliest methods of controlling the tension of a drumhead. The huehuetl is one of the most ancient forerunners of the kettledrums, as the pitch of these old-old drums was tuned to match that of the chant of the priests and warriors.

ers or chanters. It had a solemn, grave tone, which the Mexican Indian boy of today tries to imitate on a poor copy of his own making. Originally the huehuetl was played with the hands and fingers, but today the Indian boy uses two sticks on his footed drum.

The huehuetl is a close relative of the footed Assator drum of the West Indies and of Africa. The Assator drum is considered by the Afro-Haitians to be the only musical instrument that is itself a god. This belief comes from the fact that the drum is extremely sensitive. Its vibrations may be set in motion even by a gentle breeze.

The Ka of the West Indies is a large barrel-like drum with only one head. It rests horizontally on the ground while being played by one drummer who sits astride it and performs on it with his hands as he presses his right heel against the head to vary the pitch. This is called 'heeling' the drum. Another drummer beats with two sticks on the open end of the shell of the drum to complete the personnel of this one-drum band.

The *conga* (congo) drum seems to be a degenerate cousin of the huehuetl, not only in appearance, but in usage as well. 'Congo' means 'dance,' in the Nyam-nyam language of this tribe of aboriginal Africans; so the conga drum used in Latin-American rhumba bands (Afro-Latin might be a more appropriate name) is, translated into English, a *dance* drum. The Nyam-nyams, who use the congo drum, were among the most notorious cannibals of all Africa. Their name, 'yum-yum,' is derived from the sound of smacking lips at the thought of food. Although the Nyam-nyams, thoroughly ashamed of their gastronomic propensities, call themselves 'Nzangah,' an "appellation denoting the utmost contempt and disgust."*

The great age and long use of the congo drum may be attested to by the picture of a single eye one occasionally finds painted on the deep barrel-like shape of their long bodies. This 'all-seeing eye' is of great significance and antiquity, for it establishes a relationship with the very beginning of life and light.

To the drummers of old, and perhaps even to some of today, the Eye was God. It was considered to be the most potent of all things. It was both the most feared and at the same time the most desirable. Man's eye could go away from him to the clouds, the mountains, the moon, sun and stars. His hands or feet could not. The Eye was Ormadz' most potent power over man. Zarathustra made a picture of an eye, and placed it over the altar; and the Eye was placed in the soul of man to watch over him, so he could commit no wrong. The Eye was called *Conscience*.

The ancient beliefs related to the eye which may be seen painted on congo drums claim that the first living things upon Earth were without eyes. All was darkness. But when Light appeared, living things focalized toward the light, and this focus was called an 'eye.'

Such as were quickened into life, and not attached to the earth by fibres or roots, were called animals. The life they inherited gave them the power to move about and go from place to place. Those less fortunate or less advanced creations, such as plants and flowers, manifest this attraction for the Light; for even without eyes they may be

*Louis C. Elson, Curiosities of Music.

seen following the direction of light as they sit in their window pots or in the garden.

The eyes were the first organs of sense created in any animal. They are said to be the seeds of the tree of knowledge, the beginning of self-creation, and the acquirer of knowledge; and they accomplish their going forth and staying at home at the same time.

Primitive people frequently painted or carved eyes on various objects, in order that those objects might see. The Chinese gave eyes to their ships so they would not be blind and perhaps become wrecked on dangerous rocks. The Egyptians used the Eye of Horus as a talisman to guard them from evil. Certain modern religions include the magic Eye in their ritual or its setting. Ancient philosophies claimed that an All Seeing Eye was the Cause and Creator of the whole Universe, and that the Universe is the 'person' of the Creator.

Probably the use of an eye painted on the long shell of a congo drum, or on the head of certain drums used in India, had a greater significance in former times than it does now. Perhaps its current use might parallel that of the vigilant eyes painted on the strange ships of the Chinese — that the eye is there solely for the purpose of keeping the drum from making a mistake.

The beat of the tom-tom is a simple one. If we move its prosaic rhythmic throb from the ancient plains of Central Asia to the fertile prairies of North America, as the drum itself may have been moved in a bygone age, we will find that it was usually played in unison with the rhythm of the chanted words of the tribe or its medicine-man, or with the words of a song. For an accompaniment to a song the tom-tom would beat time briefly before the voices began, to set the rhythm, and then again at the end, after the singing stopped. At other times the tom-tom would beat an entirely different rhythm to that of the singing, as if striving for crude rhythmic polyphony.

The simple rhythm of the tom-tom may sometimes be developed to symphonic proportions and set a dramatic background for a whole composition. The 'Dagger Dance' from Victor Herbert's opera, 'Natoma,' is an example of the tragic spell that can be woven by the relentless rhythmic pulsations of drums expressing primitive emotions.

The music usually played on the tom-tom, as a member of a band or orchestra, however, has changed but little, if any, since its introduction into the ceremonies, arts, and habits of primitive man. The pattern of quarter notes and eighth notes remain about the same, ordinarily, and upon hearing the deep-toned rhythmic beat of this ancient drum — which, in Malaya, is called 'tong-tong' — the listener is immediately transported musically to scenes of African, Indian, or Oriental life. The instrument has nevertheless been the foundation upon which has been built other related drums, and it has provided our percussion sections with several important members.

The *bass drum*, which is merely a large tom-tom with more refined heads and a means for mechanically adjusting their tension, is one of the most important instruments to be found in either band or orchestra. Turkey is said to have contributed this valuable addition to our musical family, and until the beginning of the nineteenth century the bass drum was referred to as the *Turkish* drum.

The Turkish Drum.

As well as being one of the most expressive of instruments, the bass drum together with the cymbals, is the most dangerous. A well-meaning conductor will sometimes assign his least competent musician to play either one or perhaps *both* of these hazardous contraptions, and the results are occasionally disasterous; for an inferior musician on the bass drum or cymbals may ruin completely the work and artistry of an entire organization. It would be far better to reverse this customary practice and assign the best musicians in the band or orchestra to play these conspicuous instruments. A bass drum or cymbals played too loudly will be so out of balance that all semblance of music will be lost. If played even slightly out of rhythm, the ensemble will be ruined, and a beat in the wrong place is simply catastrophic.

While the bass drum is usually played with its heads in a vertical position, being struck with a rather soft beater of medium weight, it is sometimes turned at an angle or even placed in a horizontal position and played with two sticks, or perhaps by two players.

The proper place to strike the bass drum is relatively near the center of the head, for normal playing, using the up-stroke of a glancing blow to produce the tone. If softer playing is desired, the drum should be struck farther from the center; and for real loud passages or beats, the head should be struck quite near the center.

To muffle the drum and stop the vibrations after it has been played upon, the fingers may be placed carefully on the heads, or the stick may be used if the player is able to dampen the tone in this manner without producing another audible beat.

Occasionally harder or softer sticks may be necessary for giving the correct tone, so the bass drummer should have three or four sticks of different degrees of softness and weight; and as rolls requiring the use of two sticks alike in weight and texture are called for at times, provision should be made for this possibility.

The bass drum is an instrument of *indefinite* pitch, so the heads should be checked carefully for their tonality before it joins the ensemble. When the weather is damp the heads will relax, and their tone will be quite low and lifeless. The sound will be too long in character, and the drum will not respond properly to the touch of the player. When this occurs, the heads should be tightened until a satisfactory solid — but indefinitely pitched — beat can be produced. During dry weather the opposite will be true. The heads will shrink and the tone will become more of a dull dead thud than one sounding like the vibrant boom of a good bass drum. In this case the heads should be relaxed until the proper tone is produced. If dampness is prevalent, dark-colored electric lights of small wattage, or a regular drum heater, installed inside the drum will help keep the heads dry and better sounding. If lights or heaters of too great wattage are used, the drum heads will be 'cooked,' and in a short time become lifeless and ruined. *A good tone comes only from heads of elastic quality,* and too much heat takes the elasticity from the heads.

When tuning the bass drum, the tension rods must all be tightened or loosened as nearly the same amount as possible. Care must be exercised in setting the tension of the

heads even when the drum is not in use; for during dry
weather the heads will shrink, and if the tension is left
too slack the heads may contract to such a degree that it
will be impossible to produce low tones on them without
first wetting the heads. On the other hand, if the heads
are left for several damp days with the rods tightened, they
may stretch so much as to take all of the elasticity from
them. Drum heads should be kept fairly tight in dry weather,
and moderately loose in damp weather.

When the bass drum joined the orchestra it was considered quite a novelty. The scoring for it in Mozart's 'Seraglio'
treated the bass drum as a horizontally suspended long instrument to be played with two sticks, and the music indicated which hand to use in playing. The upper line was
to be played by the right hand and the lower line by the
left hand.

This two-handed style of bass drum playing became that
used more spectacularly later on by the Scottish bands of
drums and pipes, after the width of the drum was narrowed
from the shape it had as an Oriental instrument.

The bass drum, or 'long drum,' as it was called by Berlioz, has a very important and exciting part to play in
Verdi's 'Requiem Mass'; and in Rossini's 'Barber of Se-
ville' it has a part equally prominent as that given to the
kettledrums.

At first our musical ancestors appear to have been completely satisfied with the boom, boom, boom-boom-boom of the tom-tom, but the fascinating and cheerful tinkling sounds of the sistrum were destined to be incorporated into its vibrant throbs. Some clever inventive genius of that time of long ago conceived the idea of using jingles in the form of small cymbals, bells, and even coins fixed on the inside of his tom-tom so it would produce the jingling sound that was so dear to the ear of our early musicians and music-lovers. This new drum, which combined the tone of the tom-tom with the jingling sounds of the sistrum, became our modern *tambourine*.

The tambourine made its appearance quite independently in various parts of the world. It was invented by many widely separated peoples. In China it was a drum of about nine and one-half inches in diameter, having four pairs of metal jingles and a head of snakeskin. Those of ancient Palestine were slightly smaller, and they contained five pairs of jingles made of brass. In Persia the tom-tom was developed into a large nineteen-inch tambourine, ornamented on the outside and furnished with bells, rings, and coins on the inside. Turkey provided us with a smaller instrument, octagonal in shape, painted red, its sides decorated with mirrors, and carrying a complement of four pairs of jingles. The electrifying sound of the rattlesnake was suggested by the early Mexican tambourines, for they were made in the shape of a snake biting the head of a tortoise.

It is to Spain, or to the Basque people living in Spain, however, to whom for some unknown reason credit is given for the tambourine as it is today, and for whom the instrument was named — the 'Tambour de Basque,' or 'Drum of the Basques.' This tambourine, or *little drum*, is about ten inches in diameter. It has twelve pairs of small tinkling cymbal-like jingles fixed in its shell by means of pins running through their centers and through the shell, in which aperatures have been cut to allow a place for them.

The single head of the tambourine is fastened to the shell, or rim, by means of large-headed tacks in a manner similar to that employed by the Chinese for their tom-toms.

The tambourine is played in several different ways. It may be held in the left hand and struck with the fingers, knuckles or palm of the right hand. The fingers of the left hand may also be used on the inside of the instrument, while the right hand plays on the outside. The tambourine may be struck against the player's knee with one hand, and on the inside of it with the other, as it is bounced back and forth between hand and knee. This method is especially good for fast loud passages, such as those found in Rimsky-Korsakow's 'Scheherazade.' For more delicate execution the tambourine may be placed upside-down on a pillow and played on the rim with the fingers or with soft-headed sticks. It may be placed on a snare drum or a kettledrum for certain effects, the jingling sound of the tambourine being produced when the larger drum is struck. The thumb may be moistened on the player's tongue and then moved around the edge of the head of the 'little drum,' keeping the thumb quite stiff in order to make the jingles vibrate. A thin coating of shellac may be brushed on the outer inch or two of the head, so as to form a band around its circumference, and then sand quickly sprinkled on and allowed to dry. This will provide a sandpaper surface and will simplify making a roll on the tambourine in this manner. The roll may be made sistrum-style, by simply shaking the instrument; but for a closely-knit roll, the moistened thumb technique is more effective.

There should be at least two tambourines available for use in the orchestra. One should be equipped with thin, crimped jingles, for pianissimo passages of transparent softness, such as the few notes used in 'Danse Arabe,' from Tschaikowsky's 'Nut Cracker Suite'; and another tambourine having heavier jingles for use in more boisterous compositions.

The thin crimped jingles of the softer sounding tambourine are descended from the *faggeislah* (castanets of brass) of Syrian origin.

The heads of tambourines may be coated with clear lacquer or shellac, to make them less subject to the weather.

Tambourines and castanets have become so much a part of the characteristic music of Spain that one is likely to forget another contribution to the percussion family of instruments which has been developed in that area. This instrument is the *tambourin* (pronounced tom-bor-oń). It is the deep-toned tenor drum, a modernized tom-tom with all the mechanical improvements of the latest design, but having no snares incorporated into its construction. It is played with soft-headed sticks similar to those generally used on the kettledrums.

When the score calls for a tenor drum or a tambourin, a

large, deep-toned tom-tom is sometimes substituted.

The tambourin has a close relative in the 'provincal' drum of Spain and France. It is a smaller member of the tenor drum family.

Jules Massenet, in his 'Le Cid' Ballet, and Georges Bizet, in the 'Farandole,' from his 'Suite L'Arlesienne,' have written typical parts for the tambourin.

Often there is a misunderstanding regarding the proper instrument to use when the score calls for the tambour*in*, and a tambour*ine* is incorrectly used instead. The player or the conductor, not knowing there is a difference, presumes that the name of the instrument has been misspelled or misprinted, or that 'tambourine' is spelled differently in some other language. This, however, is a case of mistaken identity, for the *tambourin* is a deep-toned drum having no snares, while its cousin, the *tambourine*, or 'Tambour de Basque,' is a single-headed 'little drum' with metal jingles adorning its circumference.*

*In German the tambourine is spelled 'tambourin.' It may also be called the *beckentrommel*, — the 'cymbal drum.'

A primitive Congo drum with a snare.

Timbales are single-headed stick-played tom-toms used in pairs. They are unique among modern drums which have a means for tightening their heads, for a timbale does not necessarily use a counterhoop to hold its head in place. The head is sometimes mounted on a rather wide fleshhoop and then placed on the drum in an inverted position. The tensioning mechanism is positioned directly over the upper edge of the inverted fleshhoop and fastened to the shell of the drum, so it may be adjusted by means of a key.

Timbales do not have a kettle-like shape, and they are much smaller than kettledrums; but in French their name is also that of the kettledrums. It would be most unusual, however, to find both varieties of timbales used in the same composition or even in the same orchestra, owing to vast differences in their musical personalities.

Algiers has provided another very important development of the tom-tom, for there an ancient someone had the idea of fastening five gut strings across the underside of his drum's head in order to create a rattle-like sound, or perhaps to increase its volume. This addition of gut strings, or snares, to the tom-tom changed it into a *snare drum!*

There were no means for tightening the single head of this first crude snare drum, and it is quite likely that this convenient feature was not necessary in the hot dry climate of North Africa.

African tribes other than the Bendirs stretched a string of gut or rawhide over the heads of their drums in order to obtain this sound which combined the beat of the tom-tom with the vibrations of the rattle. The American Indians produced an effect similar to that of the Bendir drum of North Africa by placing short sticks on thongs of rawhide inside their tom-toms. These medicine-stick instruments made a constant tapping noise as the heads of the drums vibrated from the beats of the drumstick, and the resultant sound resembled the buzz of a rattle more than it did the sharp snap of snares.

While the Bendir drum of Algiers seems to have been the first step in the transition from the tom-tom to the snare drum, it is believed, however, that the Turks had a lot to do with its development into the form we now see. Formerly the tension of the heads was regulated by means of rope or leather 'ears' encircling V-patterned ropes threaded between them, but eventually rods of metal replaced the less efficient method of head adjustment.

In the year 675 A.D. drums were assured a place in the family of instruments to be used in the bands and orchestras yet to come, for in that year several singers in Pope Gregory's great school of music were invited from Rome to teach singing of the rare new chants of that period in the monasteries of England. At first no musical instruments were permitted to be played in the Church; but the lyre and harp were admitted eventually, and then at a later period the psaltery, cymbals and the *tabor* were accepted

Precortesian Tabor and Pipe.

in the orchestra of the Church.

The *tabor* (tambour or drum) of about the eighth century was a small light instrument. It was tied to the player's chest or to his left arm by a cord or ribbon, and it was played with only one stick held in the right hand. The reason for its being held in this manner was the fact that the drummer also played a three-holed flageolet-type instrument with his left hand, while he beat the drum and sometimes danced.

Cymbals, tambourines (tymbyr) and many kinds of drums, both with and without snares, gradually came into general use during this period.

It is of some interest to note that the tabor and pipe combination of the eighth century in Europe was also known and used by the ancient Aztecs or Mayans of Mexico in a manner quite similar to its use in England up to the time of Henry VIII, when the tabor was replaced by the larger *military drum*.

By the time of Edward the Third (1312-1377) the tabor had achieved considerable popularity, and in his household band Edward included a tabor player. King Henry Eighth (1491-1547), a great lover of music, pomp and ceremony, included four tambourines and four drums in his musical group consisting of seventy-nine musicians. Henry was especially fond of drums, and it was he who introduced the kettledrums into England. The tabor had developed in-

---

The Precortesian Tabor and Pipe of Mexico seems to have developed simultaneously with its pre-Elizabethan counterpart in England and in other parts of Europe. The present-day fife and drum corps are a continuation of this ever popular drum and flute combination of sounds.

to the *military* drum by Henry's time, and it was used during court functions, for occasions of pompous state ritual, and even as a part of the band playing the royal dinner music. The 'new sound' to dinner music, however, we are told, may be accredited to Queen Elizabeth (1533-1603), for she caused the royal table to be serenaded "quite lustily, with twelve trumpets and two kettledrums, which together with fifes, cornets, and side-drums, made the halls ring for half an hour together."

By the middle of the seventeenth century the delicate-toned tabor had completely given way to its stirring masculine relative, the *military-* or *side-drum;* and the drum with snares, played with a stick held in each hand, found a permanent place in the military routine of Great Britian, and in the events of the royal court.

The tabor, which remained without snares, was gradually enlarged into the previously mentioned tenor drum. In France (Provence) it grew into a large cylinder-type drum. Sometimes it had snares, and sometimes none. When the drum part calls for the 'tambourin a' cordes,' (the drum with cords, or snares) the *snare drum* is being asked for. The *tambourin,* or 'tambourin sans cordes,' is the deep-toned drum without snares.

Usually there is little to be misunderstood when selecting the right drum for American or British compositions which confine their requests to military drums, field drums, side drums, or just plain snare drums. But quite often those asked for by composers from other lands present some doubt to the average conductor or drummer, and occasionally the wrong instrument is used by mistake.

The use of the wrong percussion color may change the whole character of a composition, so it is important that an understanding of the various kinds of snared and unsnared drums is one of the accomplishments of the player as well as of the conductor.*

After the defeat of the Turkish armies, in 1700, their music spread throughout Europe, and their instruments — which were chiefly oboes, cymbals, triangles and drums — found their way into the instrumental family of the European symphony orchestra. In 1717 the military drum became an important part of the music and the military branches of America, too, for in that year "Drums" of the Prince of Wales' Volunteers was stationed at Annapolis, Maryland. "Drums" was the name given to a British regiment's fife, drum and bugle corps.

At that period the snare drum, or military drum, was carried by means of a sling worn across the player's right shoulder, so it would rest at his left side, and for that reason it was called a "side" drum.

The rope-tensioned snare drums of Colonial days, and of more recent times, too, consisted of a wooden shell of about twelve inches in depth, by seventeen inches in diameter. At first the rope was simply placed under and over the counterhoop, but later on the counterhoops had holes bored in them to allow a small rope to be threaded through them in an up-and-down V-pattern, each V encompassed with a constricting circle of leather for drawing the V-segments together and thereby tightening the heads. This method of head-adjustment was copied from the Turks. The

*See the Appendix to Part I for comparisons and descriptions.

heads were usually of calfskin, and the snares were made of lamb or sheep gut. Both drums and drumsticks were apt to be a product of the craftsmanship of the drummer.

The snare drum is now made in several sizes, and of both wood or metal. Those of small size may sometimes be referred to as "side drums," owing to the manner in which their predecessors were carried; while the larger ones may be called "field drums." Both kinds are basically alike, excepting in size.

When playing in a small orchestra, the drummer should use an instrument of small size equipped with coiled wire snares, so his playing will be in balance with the quality and quantity of the sound produced by the group. But a large band of brass and woodwinds requires military drums with gut snares, in order to give the music the thrilling martial air it should possess. A set of snares combining both coiled wire and gut will be found to be excellent, if properly adjusted.

One may find at times a few notes for a bell of indefinite pitch written in the drum music, and suitable bells are occasionally found attached to the counterhoop or shell of the drum with which to voice this primitive memory.

Sometimes the score will call for the snare drum sticks to be played claves-like, one against the other. This effective bit of rhythmic coloring is reminiscent of centuries gone by, when aboriginal people "hit two sticks together, or two green branches."

Appendix to Part One

CLOSE NEIGHBORS may argue over the instrument intended when the score calls for a *tambourin,* and each may be equally certain that the other fellow is wrong. One says that the tambourin is a deep-toned cylinder drum to be played with but one stick, while his colleague a few miles away insists that it is a *tambourine:* a "kleine trommel mit kleine becken"— a little drum with small cymbals.

The controversy relative to the tambourin and the tambourine is one which may be extended to include a considerable portion of the drum family. Adjacent countries have different names for the same instrument, and some slight variation in construction adds to the perplexity and makes the problem of identification a difficult one for those not thoroughly acquainted with the drums involved. In order that both the conductor and the percussionist may have expert advice when selecting unfamiliar drums, and that they also may have a better understanding of this unfortunate lack of clarity or standardization, the following descriptions and definitions are given. Two outstanding authorities on the subject of foreign drums have contributed reliable information, and to them we are deeply indebted.

First, for his descriptions of the drums most likely to be asked for when playing French scores, we may thank Mr. Leon Arnaud, composer-conductor, arranger and music-consultant for Twentieth Century-Fox Studios of Hollywood, for his helpful favor.

The *tarole,* or *caisse plate.* This is a thin, flat little drum. It is only about three inches in depth, and perhaps thirteen or fourteen inches in diameter. It is equipped with eight or more snares, preferably of gut.

Caisse claire is the regular orchestra snare drum, and it is somewhat larger than *caisse plate.* It also is equipped with eight or more snares, those of gut preferred.

The *caisse roulant* is the French equivalent of the drum known as the "field" drum in American nomenclature. It is similar to the *caisse claire,* but it is a deeper bodied drum having four or more gut snares.

The *tambourin,* or *tambour de Pro-vence,* is a very deep drum. It may be asked for "sans cordes" (without snares), or again it may be requested "avec cordes" (with snares). When snares are installed on the *tambourin* they are position-ed across the top of the batter head of the drum. Two snares of heavy gut, such as the G-string from a string-bass, are used. The *tambour-in* is played with only one short thick drumstick, and it should strike directly over the snares.

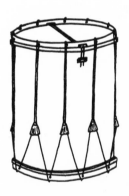

The *tambour militaire* is similar to the *caisse roulant.* It has, however, four snares of gut. They should be about the size of a 'cello D-string, and they are placed against the snare head of the drum.

Note: The accepted French style of snare drumming re-quires that the drum be played at an angle of forty-five degrees, as better results in both tone and technique are obtainable when the drum is held in that position. Both sticks should hit the center of the batter head alternately, even when playing a roll or making flams "hand to hand."

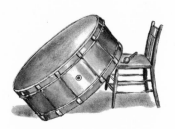

The following descriptions and comparisons are those made available through the courtesy of Herr Hermann Gschwendtner, of the Munich Philharmonic Orchestra. While the various drums may be described as being other than the American drummer may have believed them to be, it is most fortunate to have Herr Gschwendtner's exposition and the views of the German drummer on this unsettled matter of drum names and diversities of construction.

French

Originally the *caisse claire* of the French harmony-music (band) had eight tension rods and a metal shell, so it is a recent addition to the French percussion instruments. Its size has changed from 4½ by 15 inches to about 6¼ by 14 inches. *Caisse claire* is said to be an imitation of the English or American *small drum*.

Tarol Gregoire is a very old *caisse claire*. It has gut snares. Only five tension rods are installed on its shell of of brass. It measures about 8½ by 15¾ inches.

The *tambourin, or tambour provencal,* has a wooden body, which is sometimes carved. This drum uses very light, thin heads which produce a hollow dull sound. It has but one gut snare tightly stretched between the hide and the rim of the drum. It has a diameter of about 16 inches and is approximately 23 inches in depth. The *tambourin* is struck with only one stick.

Caisse roulante has no snares. It is a variation of the *tambourin,* as it formerly used a snare during the sixteenth century. (Louis XIII) Occasionally the *caisse roulante* is substituted for the *tambourin, tambour or tambour militair.* It varies in size from depths of 8 or 10 inches and diameters of about 14½ to 15¾ inches.

German

The German *Grosse Ruehrtrommel* of former times had but one drumhead, and it was without snares. In size it was about the same as the *tambourin* of France and the large English *tabor*—16 by 23 inches. When it had snares it was known as the *Landsknechttrommel.*

Near the middle of the 18th century the *Grosse Ruehrtrommel* was made in a reduced size, measuring approximately 12 by 16 inches, and snares were added. It then became known by other names: *Blaser Trommel, Wirbeltrommel,* and *Rolltrommel.* When, during this period metal bodies came into use instead of the previous wooden ones, and the rope tensioning device was replaced with threaded rods of metal, the big *Ruehrtrommel* of former days was replaced by the smaller German *military drum*. In size it varied from 5 to 8 inches in depth, and from 11 to 14¼ inches in diameter. At the beginning of the 20th century another reduction in size took place, and this still smaller new instrument with snares was given the name of *Kleine Trommel* (small drum) or *Konzerttrommel* (concert drum). It was about 7 inches deep and 14¼ inches wide. When still again the size was diminished to 5¼ by 14¼, the *concert drum* became the *Kleine Jazz Trommel* (little jazz drum). For a sharper, snappier sound, the depth of the *little jazz drum* was lessened to 4 inches, and the tiny new snare drum was christened a *"Bop" Trommel*.

English

The big English *tabor* was sometimes similar in size to the French *tambour provencal* and the *Landsknechttrommel* of Germany. Sometimes it was provided with a single snare on top of the batter head; then it was called the *tambour provencal*. When it had no snares it was the *tambourin*. Again it was made to resemble the *Landsknechttrommel,* in which case it was provided with snares on the snare head instead of on the batter head.*

Tenor drums measure about 12 by 15 or 16, or even 17 inches wide. Like the tambourin, *tenor drums* have no

*Note: The Oriental word 'tabor' is a generic term for 'drum.' It does not mean any special kind or size of drum, so tabors could be either large or small and they could be either with or without snares. Tabors, tambours, ta'bo'rs, are very closely related words.

snares. Wooden shells are customary. Originally rope tension was used, but it has been replaced with metal rods for tightening the heads. *Tenor drums* may be played either with regular heavy snare drum sticks, or with sticks having soft felt balls for striking the head.

The English *field drum, parade drum or street drum* is a drum with a wooden shell. For tightening its heads it may employ either rope or metal rods, and it is equipped with gut snares.* In size the *field drum* is slightly smaller than the *tenor drum*.

While most of the drums mentioned in the foregoing are *snare drums,* owing to the use of a snare or snares in their construction, the drum bearing the title of *"snare" drum* is a smaller instrument. Its measurements approximate 6 or 8 by 14 or 15 inches, depth and diameter, respectively. It is equipped with gut snares drawn over the snare head.**

*As this drum was the one used for parades and marching, it was carried by means of a sling, so it would rest in playing position at the drummer's side. The "field" drum was called the "side" drum for this reason.

**The upper head of the drum, the one upon which the sticks strike, is called the *batter* head. The opposite head, the vibrations of which are activated sympathetically by the beating of the sticks on the batter head, and against which the snares are placed, is called the *snare* head.

American snare drums are similar in size to English ones, but coiled wire snares, or a combination of coiled wire and gut are often used (to good advantage) for concert playing.

If the reader is not already thoroughly confused by the preceding descriptions of the drums of England, France and Germany, he may continue on to those of Italy.

The words used in Italian for drums may be either *cassa* or *tamburo*. *Cassa* literally means *chest* or *box*, but the *Gran Cassa* (big box) is the *bass drum*, in Italian musical terminology. *Tamburo* is, of course, a generic word related to *tabor* and *tambour*, and it means simply *drum*.

Tamburo vecchio (old drum) is an instrument for museums rather than for modern orchestras. The French *Tarol Gregoire* is a similar drum.

Tamburo rullante is sometimes mistakenly thought to be be a "round" drum, or one for "making rolls"; but it is instead the Italian version of the French *caisse roulante*. This drum is described as having snares by some, while again it is said to be without them. In the final analysis the musical taste and judgement of the drummer or the conductor must decide which type of instrument to use by matching its timbre with the character of the composition being played.

Tamburo militaire, the *military drum*, should fill the qualifications of a drum used in parades. It should be of good size, still not too heavy. The English *street*, or *field drum*, is the equivalent of the *tamburo militaire*.

Cassa dura is not a drum. It means that the drum (heads) should be hard (tight).

Tamburo piccolo is a small *snare drum*.

Bwongo Drums.

The author with a pair of Viennese kettledrums made about 1900. These drums tune with a masterkey; but, there being no nut nor T-screw provided for that purpose, individual tensioning of the rods requires the use of a pipe wrench or a pair of pliers. Instead of using counterhoops to hold the heads in place, U-bolts are fixed through the fleshhoops. The drums were made by Hans Schnellar, of Vienna. Photograph by Otto Rothschild.

CHAPTER V

Kettles and Pots

RESONANCE was the first musical qualification discovered by man and it has been a prime consideration ever since it was first noticed.

In his search for more resonance in his favorite and most fascinating musical instrument, primitive man found that a skin stretched tightly over a hollow cylindrical form produced the best results. Early Egyptian sculptures show drums made of skin stretched over hollowed-out logs, and these ancient mementos indicate that drums of this type had been in use long before the advent of any historical record.

Ever since its inception, the drum has remained much the same. Artistic genius through the ages has ornamented the bodies of drums with meaningful carvings and painted designs, and the heads have been decorated, or left in a significant natural state. Mechanical ingenuity has perfected ways for holding the heads, jingles, or snares in place, for adjusting them and for improving their quality and appearance. The drum, nevertheless, reduced to its simplest analysis regardless of its artistic or mechanical changes, still consists of a head or heads of skin tightly stretched over a hollow cylindrical form. The search for greater resonance, however, has never ended.

Having learned that the tone of a drum is better when its

head is stretched over a hollow cylindrical form, the early drum-makers began experimenting and searching for the means of still greater improvements in the tone of their instruments. Primitive man found that his drum had a better tone when the head was not too loose, so many ways were devised by which the tension of the head could be adjusted. Wedges or blocks of wood were forced under the lacings to keep them tight and the heads stretched. Some large tom-toms, such as the *mosque drums* of Malaya, were built so wedges would elevate the drum and tighten the strips of rawhide which connected the head to a separate stand upon which the drum rested. Probably the most unusual of these ancient tension systems was that used by the Mexicans of old, who employed the principle of the tourniquet for tightening the heads of their primitive *huehuetls*.

The search for ever better drums never ceased, and improvements were always found. Drums were made in all possible sizes, and their shapes were varied in all imaginable cylindrical and barrel-like forms. Different kinds of wood were used for the bodies of drums, and efforts were made to find more resonant drumheads. Drums were built for playing while being held in a horizontal position. Others were made to stand upright on the ground, or imbedded into it. Eventually someone tried fastening a skin over a bowl-shaped form: probably a section of a round gourd, a pottery dish, or perhaps the brain-pan of the skull of a former adversary. This hemispheric shape, a cylinder with a rounded closed bottom forming a resonator, or reflector for the sound, proved to be the most resonant shape of all. Through the long ages this type of drum has been used by many peoples. It has a name in many languages, and it is the most musical and most popular member of the entire percussion family. In English it is called the *kettledrum*.

The original home of the kettledrums seems to have been in the Middle East. Drums of this type may still be found in use today among the Indians, Arabs, Persians and Egyptians, and their neighbors. Kettledrums were in use in Germany during the sixteenth century, at which time they were known as *Persian drums*, although the first pair of such instruments are said to have been imported from Egypt. These imported Egyptian drums were a small prototype of the 'nakers.'* They measured only six and three-quarters by eleven inches for the larger drum, and four and one-eighth by eight and one-half inches for the smaller, diameter and depth respectively.

In the book of Travels written by Marco Polo,** in which he describes the great battle between Alau and Berca in 1261, we are given interesting information relative to these instruments. ". . . After the two armies had remained a short while in the face of each other, the *nacars* at length sounded, upon which both armies let fly such a shower of arrows at each other that you could hardly see the sky, and many were slain, man and horse." And again, in his description of the battle fought by King Kaidu against the armies of his uncle, the great Khan, in 1266: ". . . And when the two armies were drawn up in the field, and waited only for the signal to be given by sounding the *nacar*, they sang and sounded their instruments of music in such a man-

*'Naker' is the Anglicized version of 'nacaire' or 'nacar.'
**The Travels of Marco Polo (The Venetian), edited by Manuel Komroff.

ner that it was wonderful to hear. For the Tartars are not allowed to commence a battle till they hear the *nacars* of their lord to sound. As soon as the sound of the *nacars* was heard, the battle began, and they put their hands to their bows, and placed the arrows to the strings."

In the tales of his interesting travels, Marco Polo tells of his stay with Kublai Khan, the thirteenth century founder of the Mongol Dynasty in China, and, among many other noteworthy things, he mentions the use of kettledrums in the army, for signaling during battles. Two generations before the time of which Marco relates, Genghis Khan was busily engaged with the conquest of the world. King Genghis, 'The Ruler of All Men,' was born (as Temujin) in 1162 A.D. — the Year of the Swine, in the calendar of the Twelve Beasts — and he died in 1227, or the Year of the Mouse, in the same cycle of Beasts. Fragments of the story of this extraordinary Slayer of Men, who murdered and destroyed or stole over an area extending from Armenia to Korea, and from Tibet to the Volga River, have been recorded in various chronicles, notably among which is the saga of the Mongol Ssanang Setzet.

In these old writings occasional mention is made of things musical, which were indulged in even in the difficult nomadic life in the barren wastes of the Gobi. A short phrase alludes to 'Arghun, the lute player.' And we are told that 'before every potation' — the Mongols believed in drunkenness, but in some moderation — 'before every potation, a servant hastened out (of the yurt) to pour a libation to the quarters of the four winds,' while a tune was struck up on the one-stringed fiddles. We are told that the world of

Genghis Khan was a martial one, but still not one unappreciative of music. At dawn a drum-roll sounded for the march to begin. During the din of battle 'when the human voice could not be heard and *cymbals* and *kettledrums* might be mistaken for the enemy's instruments, signals were given by the arm movements of an officer.'

In speaking of the enemy, 'his army was several times the strength of the Mongol division, and Muhammad — beholding for the first time the dark mass of fur and feather clad warriors without shields or chain mail — thought only of launching his attack before the strange horsemen could escape. His disciplined Turks mustered in battle formation, and the long *trumpets* and *cymbals* sounded.'

At the beginning of the thirteenth century, within the cities of Cathay, there were pleasure lakes with barges where men could sit and drink wine made of rice, while they listened to the melody of silver *bells* in a woman's gentle hand.*

*Harold Lamb, Genghis Khan, The Emperor of All Men.

Mary and Adam Brown record a pair of Palestinian *nag-garah,* which are small bowl-shaped china drums with diameters of only three inches for the smaller drum and five and one-half inches for the larger.

In his History of Musical Instruments, Curt Sachs tells of the *sahib-nahabat* (master drum) used in the band of Emperor Akbar, of India. (1560-1605) These huge kettledrums were five feet in diameter, and, made of silver, they weighed four hundred and fifty pounds. Two of these big drums were carried on the back of an enormous elephant, which was draped in pompous splendor, and on the rim of each drum sat a drummer, who played it with a silver drumstick.

The *sutri-nahabat,* of the Emperor's band, as mentioned by Sachs, were smaller kettledrums having copper bowls. They were carried one on either side of a camel, which was gayly decorated with fancy trappings, and a single drummer balanced himself on the camel's back and played both drums. The camel carrying the *sutri-nahabat* in the procession of Emperor Akbar was always at the rear of the group, so one may easily imagine the loud beats and fancy flourishes of the drummer winding up the parade to have set a precedent since followed by the calliope used in circus parades of later days. It was this type of kettledrum which became known as the 'cavalry' drum in Europe, and which eventually found its way into the music of the West.

Some of the early kettle-shaped drums used by the tribes of India were made of pine wood hollowed out into hemispheric form and then equipped with heads of bull hide. Inside the wooden shell of these ancient Hindu drums were fitted bells of bronze. The drum was held high in the air and beaten in a loud and terrifying manner during battles, for the purpose of frightening the enemy. The bells were jingled by hitting against the side of the drum. This was thought to create magic and bring good luck and victory.

Tribes other than the ancient Hindus used drums instead of trumpets in warfare. "The Persians," according to Plutarch, "have no horn or trumpet to give signal of battle, but they use a certain big basin, covered with leather. They strike it on every side, and cause it to render a hollow and terrible sound, similar to thunder." It was a custom in Persia for the noblemen to use a small kettledrum while hunting eagles. When entering a forest, the drum would be beaten violently to frighten the eagles and cause them to fly and become targets for the hunters.

While some were designed to be used singly, kettledrums have been used in pairs since remote times. The earliest illustration of them is thought to be that appearing in the eleventh edition of the Encyclopaedia Brittannia.* This illustration, taken from a manuscript of Genesis dated from the fifth or sixth century, shows a woman playing four small bowl-shaped drums which are placed on a table before her. The use of four of these drums must have been exceptional, however, as they were more commonly used in pairs.

*Percival Kirby, The Kettledrums.

NAGGAREH, nacar, nacaire, naker, tambour, tambale, tabale, tabl, tympan. These are the words used for the drum during the Middle Ages. 'Tympan' is derived from Latin, 'tympanum'; but the other names come from the Arabic words: 'tambur,' 'tubal' and 'naggareth.' 'Attabal,' the Spanish word for the kettledrums, is a continuation of the ancient form, 'tabl.' This type of drum was introduced into Spain when that country was under Moorish rule, and the Moorish name has survived.

About the middle of the thirteenth century the tabl became better known in Europe through knowledge gained during the Crusades. The tabl then became the naggareth, nakkereh, neggareth, or *nacaires,* in French, and this was soon to be Anglicized into *nakers.* The French later changed to another form of the early names, and the nacaires were called 'timbales' when they developed into more musically voiced instruments.

The nakers attained great popularity in England. Some were played singly; but sometimes in pairs, too, which were attached to the waist of the drummer. Larger pairs were placed on the ground or carried on horseback and played after the fashion of the camel-carried sutri-nahabat. Nakers became a symbol of aristocracy, and they were used primarily by the nobility for ostentatious display, or for martial purposes: to increase the sound and turmoil of battle and to confuse the foe. These small kettledrums were known in Europe as early as the thirteenth century; but it was not until 1457 that the larger ones, which were the forerunners of the modern *tympani* were seen for the first time in western Europe.

In the year 1457 a party of Hungarian ambassadors was sent to France to treat for the hand in marriage of Princess Madeline, the daughter of King Charles VII, and accompanying these delegates of King Ladislaus Posthumus of Hungary were a pair of "drumes lyke bigge ketels, caryed one on each syde of ye horse's necke," such as had never before been seen. These big kettles, carried on horseback and played with the pretended luxurience of style that was a major part of their early use, so impressed those attending this meeting of high nobility that tales of the unusual fascinating drums soon spread throughout Europe. They were introduced into Germany about the beginning of the sixteenth century, where the name 'tympana' was given to the "big army kettledrums, which the princes have at court."

In 1542, or almost a century after they were introduced at the court of France, King Henry VIII of England sent to Vienna for a pair of these interesting new large drums. By 1683 they seem to have come into general use as cavalry drums, and as early as 1735 instruction books were available for teaching the "Heroic and Musical Art of the Trumpet and the Kettledrum." The first books of drum instruction dealt primarily with the various ways the kettledrummer should pose, turn and move his body with affected 'artistic' elegance; and a good drummer was one who could strike the drum with such exquisite grace that it would be ridiculous elsewhere.

When the kettledrums were first introduced into eastern Europe, possibly through contact with the Mongol hordes of the Gobi, they were still in their crude ancient Asiatic form. They consisted of heads of skin held over copper kettles by means of skin lacings fastened to the opposite side, after passing underneath the bowl. The drums' tones were either high or low, and, as they were used for rhythmical figurations of indefinite pitch, loud noise and the ostentatious flourishes and tricks of the drummer, this was of no great consequence. As late as 1636, drums of this type were still in use, but soon after they were introduced into Germany, some very essential changes were made.

The first of the changes which started the kettledrums on their way to become recognized musical instruments was the use of a hoop on which to mount the head, and another hoop of metal to hold it in place. This metal *counterhoop* had several screws placed around it, and these could be tightened or loosened to change the pitch of the tone. The screws, some fourteen or sixteen around each drum, did not have handles on them, but they were turned with a separate key. This arrangement did not allow great possibilities in tuning, but it did convert the colorful kettledrums from mere rhythmic instruments of indefinite pitch into the musical family of definite pitch.

The conversion of the ancient 'Persian' drums into cavalry kettledrums and then into the modern ones of today has been but a continuation of primitive man's search for better instruments. The use of fourteen or sixteen handle-less screws with which to adjust the tension of the drumhead has seen many improvements. Early in the nineteenth century wing-nuts or handles were attached to the tuning screws, for faster manipulation, and their number was reduced first to eight and then to six. The size of the drums was increased, too, and the relatively small pair of eighteen and twenty-four inch drums that had so greatly impressed Europe were made in sizes approximating twenty-five and twenty-eight inches.

Before the nineteenth century had ended, musically-minded inventors from all over Europe were building mechanically tuned kettledrums. At first these drums were not successful, for an adequate means for adjusting the head independently of the pedal was not provided. Finally, however, when handscrews were used to tune the head with itself, and a master-key for an overall raising or lowering of the pitch was incorporated into the mechanism of the pedal, the kettledrums became definitely and permanently regular members of the symphony orchestra.

The Early Tympanist.

IF ONE WERE to refer to illustrations depicting the early tympanist at work, hard wooden hammers in hand, arms raised high in the air and appearing as if about to administer the final blow that would forever end the annoyance of a mortal enemy, it would be easy to imagine what the first kettledrums must have sounded like. A "soune lyke thunder." That was the characteristic and accepted tone of the drums, and most composers of serious music felt that these noisy instruments were for outdoor performances only. The composers of those days who could see or hear any semblance of musical quality in "these enormous rumbling pots of the devil" and include for them a part in their scores, must have had utter disregard for public opinion and the music critics.

Nevertheless, by 1655 compositions were appearing with parts to be played by the kettledrums. Some pieces went so far as to be written for several kettledrums alone, but usually they were to be played with an ensemble of trumpets. At times the music was for three trumpets and a pair of drums; or, if the parts called for four trumpets, the drums could play the part written for the fourth trumpet, as those parts were identical and interchangable.

Ever since the kettledrums were introduced into Europe there had been a close relationship existing between the drums and trumpets. They belonged to the same guild of artists and were governed by the same laws. The music they played was alike in style and purpose. The kettledrummers of the seventeenth century even used some of the technical terms of the trumpeters in their playing, and single-sticking or double-sticking was instead called single- or double-*tonguing.*

Scorning the consequences which might result from his rash musical judgement, Jean Baptiste Lully included a part for the kettledrums in his opera, 'Thesee,' which was produced in Paris in 1675. Music for the drums had begun to appear a decade before the production of 'Thesee,' but this was the first time they had been introduced into an orchestra playing serious music.

In 1692, Henry Purcell wrote an important part for the kettledrums in his opera, 'Fairy Queen.' Both John Sebastian Bach and George Frederick Handel used the drums for creating rhythmic stability in their orchestra, but Handel's later treatment of them shows that he appreciated both their dramatic and rhythmic values. Few composers who have followed this great master have written more effectively for the kettledrums than did Handel. The 'Hallalujah Chorus' from his 'Messiah' remains one of the most thrilling and effective parts ever written for the kettledrums, and it is one of the best examples of writing for the *character* of these instruments.

The early classical composers learned that music written for the kettledrums required an entirely different treatment than did the melodic instruments. They found, by experience and observation — and good taste — that the intervals played on the drums sounded better and with more musical force when they were treated as a cadence of widely separated high and low tones, rather than as closely related melodic intervals. They learned that rapidly played rhythmic figurations became a jumbled mass of sound and gave the listener the impression that a roll was being played. They learned, in short, the *character* of the drums and how to write effectively and sensibly for them.

When the kettledrums first became a member of the orchestra they were hampered by other factors besides the use of harsh-sounding wooden or ivory-tipped sticks. One was the inadequate size of the kettles, for they were built like those designed to be carried on horseback and played in cavalry regimental groups, where the range of the drums and beauty of tone were not important. These small drums of eighteen and twenty-four inch diameters were not suited for playing notes in any but the extreme high register, and the falseness of the poor quality of the drumheads of a century or two ago made even worse the improperly placed tonality of the drums. With good modern heads on drums of such small size, the notes assigned to them would sound better if they were at least a fifth higher than those written for the kettledrums doing the pioneer work in the orchestra.

The early scores called for drums tuned to A and D, or to G and C, as it was thought that fourths were the most suited interval for them to play. Both Haydn, who was a kettledrummer, and Mozart began writing in fifths as well as fourths. Although Handel made some attempt at writing the notes for the drums on their proper lines and spaces, the custom was to name the key in which the drums were to play, and then write the music as if they were to play G and C, bass clef, instead. This gave the kettledrums the classification of 'transposing' instruments, and samples of this method of writing may still be met with in some of the older compositions. After the drums began to be given both fourths and fifths to play, this sometimes reversed the tonal placement of the instruments and became so confusing that soon thereafter the notes to be played were written on the proper lines and spaces of the musical staff.

As good taste and musical awareness increased during those formative years, the drums increased in size, too. Records show that pairs of drums thirty-nine and thirty-five inches in diameter were built, then some measuring forty-seven and forty-three inches; but these large sizes must have proved equally deficient in tonal quality and register. Neither were they found to be practical, for it was almost impossible to obtain heads big enough to fit these huge copper bowls.

Aside from the records which tell of such drums having been built, it is possible to substantitate the fact by noting the widening range of the notes called for in the scores of the early composers. This progression may be followed in the works of Beethoven, for it was during his time that the size of the drums and their corresponding range increased. The tonal requirements of the drums used by Beethoven in his nine symphonies deviate from the usual G or A on the larger drum and C or D on the smaller in his Third Symphony, for then the larger drum is tuned in B-flat and the smaller drum in E-flat. In the Sixth, Eighth and Ninth Symphonies the larger drum plays a *low* F-natural; and in the Seventh, Eighth and Ninth, the smaller drum is given a *high* F-natural to play.

During Beethoven's time (1770-1827) the kettledrums achieved a range of one octave – F to F – and from this fact alone it is safe to assume that the drums had increased in size from the original eighteen and twenty-four inch diameters to pairs measuring approximately twenty-five and twenty-eight or twenty-nine inches. A twenty-nine inch kettledrum was needed to produce a low F-natural of good quality, and one of twenty-five inches in order to play the high F. The older drums of smaller diameter could have produced this high note, but for the necessary fullness of tone in both ends of its register, a kettle of about twenty-five inches is required.

Musical scores of today sometimes call for kettledrums ranging from low C-natural below the staff to high B-flat above, — almost two octaves; but the most musical and effective tones of the drums still remain right where Beethoven left them: between F and F on the staff of the bass clef.

While experimenting with the building of larger drums in order to gain a greater range and better tonal qualities, the makers discovered that a fuller tone could be gotten from a comparatively deep kettle than from a shallow, less hemispheric one. Shallow drums tend to bring out the fundamental pitch of the principal note of the drum, but deeper kettles increase the resonance and volume of sound. Modern makers prescribe that the shape of the kettle be as deep as one-half of its diameter plus four inches.

Discovery was made, also, that unless a small hole is provided in the bottom of the kettle, a sharp blow with the drumstick may break the head; for when the head of the drum is struck and forced down, there must be a passageway for the displaced air to escape.

During the process of building drums of different sizes and proportions, another important requirement of kettles was learned: that in order to produce a fine tone, the rim of the bowl must be perfectly round in circumference and it must be absolutely flat on top. If the bowl were inverted and then placed on a smooth level table or bench, the perfect kettle would fit so exactly and snugly on the surface upon which it rested, that no trace of indentations or unevenness in its rim could be seen.

One experimenter found he could eliminate the overtones of his drums by cutting a small three- or four-inch hole in the center of their heads. Although this bit of surgery has merit, few tympanists attempt it for fear of ruining costly drumheads.

A celebrated inventor of musical instruments went so far as to conclude that the kettles were superfluous, that nothing was needed but the heads; and so sure was he of his theory that he drew plans for and patented a pair of kettledrums without kettles.

There have been many innovations and improvements incorporated into the kettledrums since the days of Antoine Sax. Besides being tunable with handscrews, pedals, cranks or levers, they now may be tuned by means of cables, bicycle-chains, or universal-joints. But the remarkable improvement in the sound of the drums is due largely to the better quality to be found now available in drumheads and in drumsticks.

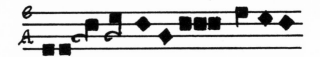

THE HISTORY of music notation could furnish interesting material for an entire book. Its development from the vaguest indication of pitch and rhythmic form to the current placement of definite tones in relation to the lines and spaces of the staff, and the precise arithmetical value assigned to them, has made possible the advancement of Music to its present importance. The unsung genius who, during the tenth century, invented the system which has grown into the notation used today, deserves credit for the greatest of all contributions to the art of sound in rhythm. Unfortunately, his name is not known.

When the first attempts at writing music began, notes had no exact value; they were simply either *short, of medium duration, or long.* There were no bar lines nor *measures;* and a sketchy indication of the desired pitch in relation to a straight horizontal line or two furnished the singer with but a meager idea of the notes and their rhythmical value. As musical awareness continually increased, however, the first crude attempts at notation were necessarily changed into a system in which each note on the staff has a definite sound as related to pitch, and a precise rhythmical value in fractions. In order to make this method of musical control workable, each group of pre-named note values were placed between bar lines for 'measuring' time; each measure containing a certain number of a specific kind of notes or their arithmetical equivalent, as stated in a Time Signature in the form of a numerator and a denominator.

At first the *shape* of the various notes suggested their relative length or brevity; but when the system based on whole or fractional notes came into use, the notes became round and either of solid black or with clear centers. 'Flags' were attached to the tail of the notes to show their musical value in fractions. Each flag added to the tail of a note decreased its value by one-half: a quarter note with a flag added to its tail became an eighth note, with two flags it was only a sixteenth note, with three a thirty-second note, and so on.

A long series of singly written fractional notes proved to be extremely difficult to read and to segregate into beats:

But the problem was solved by the invention of 'beams' to tie small groups of notes together and show a relationship of all notes to be played during the length of a rhythmic beat.

Beams were next to be used as abbreviations: a whole note with a single beam above or below it (corresponding to a single flag) meant that eight eighth notes were to be

played. A note with two beams indicated that it should be
interpreted as sixteenths. Three flags stood for thirty-second notes, so a half note (for instance) with three beams
placed across its tail or stem came to be played as sixteen
thirty-second notes.

The first music for the kettledrums left much of the actual
translation of the part to the artistic sense and musical
feeling of the player. Rolls were not indicated. Neither
beams nor *trill* signs were used. Later on, however, the use
of beams was adopted into the music written for drums, and
a triple beam over or under a note then not only indicated
thirty-second notes, it became the symbol for rolls, too.*

Occasionally the music for kettledrums contains 'measured' rolls, or rolls with their individual beats written as
notes of small denomination, or with them abbreviated by
the use of beams. This double duty assigned to beams –
their serving in the capacity of an abbreviator and also as
the sign of a roll – has caused no little confusion to the
players of the past, and it still continues to do so. An example of this ambiguous scoring may be found in Oberon
Overture, by Karl Maria von Weber, for in the Introduction
three-beamed quarter notes must be played as thirty-sec-
onds, while later on, in the Allegro, the three beams indicate a roll. The final whole note in the last bar of the Overture is not marked with either beams or a trill sign, so there

*In certain tempi the roll of drums does conform to a thirtysecond note
pattern; but in very fast movements the beats of a roll may be sixteenth
notes, or perhaps only eighths. The snare drum at a normal tempo produces a roll of thirtysecond notes. The bounced beats of sixteen sixteenth notes of a bar of Common Time fit perfectly into the thirtysecond
note pattern of a three-beamed whole note.

The small size of the drums. The hard, unmusical sticks. The false heads. The experimental nature of the parts to be played. The weather. The hall. The conductor. These were not the only things to plague the player of kettledrums up to the middle of the seventeenth century, for it could not rightly be determined whether he was a *kettledrummer* or a *tympanist!* Italy was a cultural center at that time, and the most desirous place to study music and art. Many aspiring persons left England to study in Rome, and they became so Italianized during their pleasant stay in that fabulous city that they returned to their homes with Italianized names. Joe Cooper became Giuseppe Coperario. Leo Stokes came back as Leopoldo Stokesini. The kettledrums became 'tympani,' and the kettledrummer a 'tympanist.' This fad lasted until about 1660, when the drums again became kettledrums; but the player is still more often referred to as a 'tympanist.'

An African kettle-shaped tom-tom made of wood.

A KETTLEDRUM consists of three parts: a kettle, a head, and a mechanical means for holding the head in place and tuning it. The kettle serves as a resonator or sound chamber. Its size and shape have an important relationship to the sound the head will produce. If the kettle is a shallow hemispheric bowl, the tone will be more definite in pitch; but it will have a small thin tone — one that will 'choke' and lack resonance in loud passages. If the kettle is a deep, round-bottomed cylindrical form, the sound, though harder to tune, will be of a better, more vibrant quality and it will have more volume than a shallow kettle would produce. The tone, however, can never be better than the head of the drum is able to give; for *no drum is ever any better than its head*.

From their early form consisting of a kettle-shaped bowl over which was held a skin by means of lacings or crude mechanical devices, kettledrums now offer the player a choice of several styles or models from which to choose. Unfortunately, while each type may have certain features to recommend it, no one drum can be said to be perfect in all respects. It is a matter of personal preference and intended use which the tympanist must consider when selecting a pair or a set of kettledrums.

Pedal-tuned instruments are the most convenient to play, from a tuning standpoint; for it is possible to immediately raise or lower the pitch of the drum while playing, should it be out of tune. By first having the desired pitch fixed in his ear, the player can easily get that note by touching a lower tone on his drumhead and then quickly raising the tone to it. His ear will tell him when the right pitch is reached, for he will be able to hear it ascending to the sound he has in mind, while the pedal is being depressed.

Some pedals are harder to use than others, owing to their shape or to the awkward angle they are attached to the drum, in relation to the player's position. Some pedal-drums allow the kettle to be turned to the best spot for playing, while others do not. Some drums permit their height to be adjusted to the playing position of the tympanist; others do not. Some pedal-drums have a master-key by which to raise or lower the overall pitch of the head and thereby put the pedal in a position so its arc of travel will cover the necessary range of the instrument; other drums must accomplish this adjustment by turning each tuning-screw individually. This not only takes considerable time; but, if hurriedly done, it might result in falseness in the head caused from unequal turning of the tuning-screws.

Pedal drums with their mechanism on the outside of the kettle are thought to have better tonal qualities than those having their tuning apperatus on the inside, but they are usually extremely heavy and unwieldy.

The type of pedal drums made in America are easier to use than those having originated elsewhere; but these are not perfect in every respect. Some are said to bind, or slip, or be noisy, or toneless — claims which have as their basis a certain amount of fact, perhaps, but which also may be due somewhat to a lack of mechanical understanding and thoughtful care.

Another type of kettledrum utilizes a screw principle for tuning. In order to change the pitch of drums of this kind, the kettle is revolved. This causes the playing height to vary, as the drum travels up or down on the screw; and in turning the drum to the desired pitch, no regard for the best spot on the head for sound can be paid. Should the drum become slightly out of tune while playing, it will have to remain that way until the part allows an opportunity for readjustment by hand during several bars rest.

One type of kettledrum is tuned by a single hand-operated screw, similar to the master-key of the Dresden-type drums. This single-keyed Viennese drum has no interior mechanism. It has a deep body and produces a fine tone, but tuning is not as easily accomplished as with pedal-tuned drums.

Machine drums* operated by a single crank adjust the tension of their heads by turning a handle instead of a master-key. They may or may not have their tuning mechanism on the inside of the drum, so it may or may not interfer with the tone quality.

Drums tuned by cables or bicycle chains have the tension of their heads regulated in a similar way; but instead of applying or relaxing pressure on the head by means of a pedal, a cable or a bicycle chain encircles the drum as a unit, each tuning-rod being engaged through the use of a pulley or sprocket which is turned by the movement of the cable or chain. When the handles on one or two tuning-rods are turned by hand, all the rods are turned equally by the cable or chain arrangement. Unless a flat-pitched thread is used on the tuning-rods, the high notes will be difficult to reach, as considerable strength is needed to turn them in that position.

---

*Mechanically operated tympani are sometimes referred to as *machine* drums.

Drums tuned by universal joints are operated in a similar manner, each tuning-station being governed by one of a series of connecting universal joints, all of which move when a tuning-handle is turned.

Drums of the types mentioned – cables, chains and universal joints – have nothing inside of them to deaden their vibrations, so, with a good head, they have a fine tone and adequate volume. Though not as easily tuned as pedal-equipped drums, they are much more simple to operate than drums of the handscrew type.

Kettledrums of the handscrew type, which have neither pedals, levers, cranks, chains, cables, master-keys, nor universal joints, are the simplest form of the modern kettledrum. They have, instead of a convenient system of overall tuning, six or eight single-tuning T-screws placed equidistant apart around the circumference of the drum. Each T-screw is turned individually, not only to tune the head with itself, (as is done on machine operated drums), but to raise or lower its overall pitch as well.

Tuning drums with handscrews is quite difficult. It may take several years of intimate association and contact with the technical and mechanical problems involved, to establish an acquaintance with the drums and their ideosyncrasies; but it is a method of learning which is highly recommended for the serious beginner. The difficulties to be met while playing handscrew drums will provide him with a knowledge of the kettledrums and their traits that cannot otherwise be gained. These are the drums that every aspiring arranger, composer and conductor should be required to play as part of his preparatory studies, for then he would better understand the instruments and their possibilities, and then and then only would they be treated more intelligently and effectively.

The tone of properly tuned handscrew kettledrums is full and free, and with good heads they are excellent in all respects – in all respects, with just one exception: they are the most difficult to tune.

While the relative tonal properties of the various types of kettledrums have noticable differences, for all general purposes these are not the most important considerations when selecting drums for purchase. Under certain conditions it might be necessary to have drums with an overwhelming booming sound. At other times this very superabundance of tone could be detrimental. For symphony concerts with orchestras consisting of a hundred players, a great volume of sound is needed; but when playing with smaller ensembles or for recording, the tremendous sound of the kettledrums is usually not desired. The additional vibrancy of 'good' drums is sometimes a hindrance which may have to be counteracted with the use of hard tympani-sticks.

Almost any make or model of the modern kettledrum will sound acceptably well if it is equipped with a good head properly tuned and played on with suitable sticks, unless the acoustical properties of its surroundings kill its tone, as often is the case.

Tuning Gauges

WHILE MANY PROFESSIONAL tympanists do not use them on their kettledrums, tuning gauges are of great assistance to the player. Many times a tympani part will call for important tuning changes with no time to listen for the required new tone. Such tunings, usually the product of a writer whose knowledge of the instrument is not all that it should be, are difficult to make accurately, no matter what type of drums are being used. There are times when the tympanist will have to be playing with both hands on one drum while he tunes another with his foot, and then he must play immediately on the newly tuned drum without first having an opportunity to check its changed pitch. The ultimate success of tuning depends upon the player's skill and ear, but there are many times and situations in which a pre-set note indicated on a tuning gauge would remove some of the guesswork from finding the desired pitch in a hurry.

Most pedals require so little movement when tuning short intervals that it is almost impossible to move them the small fraction of an inch needed to reach the exact spot in their travel to produce the desired note *in tune*. Larger intervals require so much more movement in comparison that fear of moving the pedal too far creates another hazard, especially in compositions containing abrupt modulations and quick changes of pitch. A reliable tuning gauge is an absolute necessity in such situations.

Tuning gauges would be especially beneficial in schools, too, and for all young players who have not yet learned to tune their drums efficiently. The tuning gauges could be pre-set on the drums by the instructor; the student-player then needs only to move the tuning mechanism to the proper place for the note required, and the change of pitch will be accomplished without fuss or guessing. In time this foundation will prove to be a great help in developing the student's ear.

Unfortunately, there are not at present many satisfactory tuning gauges for purchase on the market. One type of available indicator is attached to the kettle of the drum, just under the counterhoop. As the head moves up or down, while the drum is being tuned, pressure is exerted or relaxed on an upright rod, upon which the hoop rests. This rod in turn operates a gear, attached to which is an indicator. The indicator travels in an arc as the gear is rotated, and a pointer at its end tells the pre-set pitch at different tensions of the head. The course covered by the swing of the indicator has movable note-tabs set along its way. These are pre-set by test-tuning the drum before it is to be played in a composition; so, after its tunings have been located on the various tensions of the head and marked on the 'keyboard' by positioning the note-tabs, the drum's pitch will be registered with each movement of the hoop. Should the atmosphere become drier or damper, the drum must then be tuned again by ear to the desired note, and the indicator note-tab moved on its arc to agree with the pitch of the drum; or the indicator pointer may be disconnected and then re-set opposite the note sounded. This motion-amplifying gear type of tuning gauge, which utilizes the very slight movement of the raising or lowering of the drum's counterhoop to activate it, may be installed on any kettledrum.

Drums using either cables or bicycle-chains for tuning have a very simple method to use for pitch indication. A link in the chain, or a place on the cable is marked by a spot of bright paint or with a piece of string. A desired note is tuned on the drum, and opposite the mark on the cable or chain the name of the note is written in chalk on the drumhead.* All notes to be used in an act or a portion of a concert may be pre-tuned and marked on the drum in this way.

Kettledrums employing universal joints would have to use the pressure type, hoop-motivated gauges, as would those tuned by means of cranks, levers, or by a master-key.

Pedal-tuned kettledrums offer the best opportunity for the use of pitch indicators, as the movement of the gauge can be connected to the axle of the pedal, or directly to the pedal itself, and thereby give full advantage of its entire travel from the lowest to the highest note. Drums of the Dresden type have been equipped with tuning gauges using this principle for many years, and it is easily adaptable to any pedal-operated kettledrum of American make.

The gauge uses the rotating action of the pedal-rod, on Dresden drums, but the up-and-down motion of a pedal may be utilized for the same purpose. Should the drum become slightly flat or sharp while in use, the master-key of the Dresden-type drums is used to regulate the head so it will again match the pre-set notes on the gauge. Drums without a master-key must be re-tuned by hand until the pitch of

*If the player is using drumheads made of plastic, a china-marking pencil may be used for this purpose.

the head corresponds to the note indicated by the pointer on the keyboard of the tuning gauge.

In its simplest analysis, the tuning gauge may be said to consist of a rod which moves up and down with the action of the pedal, and a pivoted indicator activated by this motion, which points to adjustable pre-set notes.

Tuning devices can never replace a good ear, but they can greatly reduce the difficulties of tuning and lessen the worries and guesswork of even a competent tympanist.

Building a practical and efficient tuning indicator of wood or metal is not beyond the ability of most mechanically-minded drummers or instructors; so, for those who may be interested, further hints for a gauge building project are to follow.

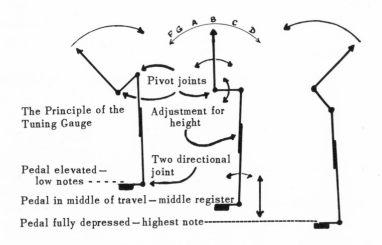

THE MECHANISM of a pedal-tuned kettledrum is such that whenever the pedal is depressed or elevated, the head of the drum is correspondingly tightened or its tension is relaxed. When the pedal is fully depressed, the drum will be tuned to the highest part of its tonal range. When the pedal is set approximately in the middle of its up-and-down movement, the head will be tuned to the middle of its compass in pitch. When the pedal is released and allowed to raise, through the contracting force exerted by the elasticity of a tensioned drumhead, the sound will be in the lower portion of the register of the drum.

In making a tuning indicator or gauge, for either amateur or professional players, the problem presented is to build a device which will translate the position of the pedal into terms of musical pitch. This may be done by utilizing a simple gadget which requires only the use of a plain pivoted piece of right-angled wood or metal, one arm of which is attached to the pedal, while the other serves as a pointer to indicate the position of the pedal.

The arm is attached to the pedal by means of an adjustable rod or strip of hardwood. It moves up and down with the pedal, and is the *control arm*. The other arm, which moves to the right or left as the pedal is moved, is the *pointer*, for in its motion it will point to the name of the note shown by the position of the pedal. The control arm must be given consideration relative to the distance its end will move, and this will be governed by its length. The requirement being that the travel of the control arm at the point of attachment to the rod which connects it to the pedal is the same distance as that covered by the pedal from its lowest to its highest position. This distance may vary in different drums; but it is about five or six inches, *approximately* one-half of which should serve as a radius for the pivoted control arm.

The length of the pointer is not critical, but the greater its length, the farther apart will be the different letters on the *keyboard* which indicates pitches or notes set on the arc traveled by the pointer.

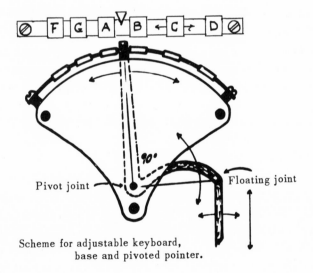

Scheme for adjustable keyboard,
base and pivoted pointer.

The *principle* of a tuning indicator has now been shown — how the movement of a pedal can be carried to a pointing arm which tells the position of the pedal, and which at the same time indicates the corresponding pitch of the drum at different tensions of the head. However, to make the gauge complete, there must be a means of calibrating the arc in which the pointer is made to travel, and in that manner translate the position of the pointer on the arc into the names of notes playable on the drum. In order to do this, the governing right-angled arms must be attached to a suitable V-shaped piece of wood or metal by a pivot fixed in the logical central point near the bottom.

The upper part of the base supporting the pivoted arms is curved to coincide with the arc followed by the pointer, and its length will be determined by the length of the pointing arm. Using the pointer as a radius, ninety degrees or slightly more of arc will be found adequate. A small flat piece of hard brass or similar metal about one-eighth of an inch in thickness, one-half inch wide and long enough to extend slightly beyond the arc traveled by the pointer, is then bent to a curved shape to match that of the arc. This is the *keyboard* of the gauge.

Movable note-tabs will next be placed around the curved metal strip in such a manner that they may be moved sideways and adjusted to the position indicated by the pointer for a specific note. A hole is drilled near each end of the curved metal piece, and after the note-tabs are installed around it, it is ready to be attached to the top of the base. Two tubular washers (spacers) about one-fourth of an inch long hold it clear of the base in order that the tabs may move freely.

The adjustable note-tabs, which have the names of the notes painted or stamped on them, are made from strips of thin metal. This metal must be stiff enough to hold its shape when bent around the keyboard. If it is too flexible it may lack springiness and will not stay in place when set opposite the pointer. Metal that is too stiff will not bend without breaking.

As many modern kettledrums have a range of a sixth or more, when suitable heads are used, six note-tabs should be formed for each drum. For a twenty-eight inch kettledrum the tabs should be from F to D, and for a twenty-five inch drum they should be from B-flat to G. The half-tones will be between the named notes.

After the tabs are in place and the race on which they move is attached to its base, the upper end of the pointer is given a suitable shape and angle, so its position may be clearly seen from above.

Any one of several ways of attaching the base and its mechanical tuning guide to the drum may be used. It may be held firmly by means of straps or springs fastened to the two tuning rods between which it rests, or the entire device may be built as an individual unit connected to the pedal, but not to the drum. If the base is to be attached to the drum, rather thick wood should be used, and it should be furred or spaced to fit the contour of the kettle. As the connecting rod must be in line with the pedal and also with the control arm, the furring or spacing must give the keyboard the correct angle of slant. A cord may be attached to the bottom of the base and fastened around the post

of the drumstand. This will keep the mechanism firmly
in place.

A Bronze Kettledrum.

CHAPTER VI

Drum Heads for Tympani

ALTHOUGH THE DRUM has become established as an instrument of cylindrical form with a skin stretched at one end or both, it is highly probable that the first drums had no shell nor form of any kind, and that they consisted of only a framework of stakes or poles upon which a freshly removed animal skin was placed and stretched for the purpose of drying.

The idea of a stretched skin without wooden support was found among many aboriginal peoples. The American Indian used a taut dried rawhide as a drum. A large stiff skin of buffalo, bear or moose was held by a circle of enthusiastic players, each one vigorously beating the skin with a stick held in one hand while pulling it tightly with the other. For a drum, the Chippewas drove stakes into the ground and stretched a skin between them. Rolls of dried kangaroo hide were used as drums by the Australian savages, and bundles of dried skin used as drums were reported by the first travelers in Africa. Some Indian tribes tied large dried skins into rolls, upon which they beat with two flat sticks.

Ages before the ancient Chinese tanned pigskins for use as drumheads, crude untanned rawhides served that purpose; and the skins of many animals, fish, reptiles and

The Mosque Drum of Malaya uses wedges of wood driven between the drum and its stand to tighten the head.

The Mosque Drum of Malaya.

even men were used for the heads of tom-toms during former millenniums of human residence upon the planet Earth.

Drumheads have improved a thousand fold since ancient man first scraped the flesh and hair from the hides he used for his drums. The greatest improvements have come quite recently, though, when modern methods replaced the primitive ones used until almost yesterday. Greater knowledge of skins and their requirements as drumheads, combined with more skill and better facilities for making them, now provides excellent ones for today's drummer.

There are two types of skins most generally used for drum heads. Occasionally, for the less demanding members of the drum family, goatskins may be found as heads for tom-toms and bongos, or porpoise skins for snare drum heads; but the best heads for snare drums, bass drums and tympani usually are made from calfskin or slunk calfskin. Young animals from two to eight weeks of age furnish skins for the batter side of snare drums; but for bass drums and kettledrums the calves must be from three to eight months old, for such heads need be stronger and of a deeper tone than skins from younger animals would provide.

A 'slunk' skin is one from an unborn calf. It is thin and smooth. Its unblemished texture is more suited for the snare side of a snare drum, as it is very resilient and responsive to the vibrations caused by the sticks beating on the batter head. A regular calfskin may produce two or three snare drum heads, or one bass drum or tympani head, on account of its larger size and thickness; but a slunk skin is so small that only one snare drum head may be cut from a whole skin.

When primitive man made drumheads from the hides of animals, he first buried the skin in the ground for several days in order to allow the flesh to rot and the hair to loosen. Today a modern machine removes the excess flesh, after which the skin is thoroughly washed and then placed in a weak lime bath for from seven to ten days. The lime solution is used for the purpose of removing the hair from the cells of the skin more easily, and to bleach the color pigment and stains from the surface. Before the skins for drumheads are dried, this solution of lime must be neutralized and the bleaching process completed. The skins are then again thoroughly washed and tacked on wooden frames and allowed to dry under ideal conditions of thermostatically controlled temperature and regulated humidity. After the skins are completely dried they are removed from the racks and then marked and cut to their most suited sizes.

There is a natural variation in the thickness of skins, so each drumhead must be shaved by hand to uniformity, and then buffed until it is smooth. The age of the animal determines the gauge of the drumhead which is made from its hide. The older a calf grows, the thicker becomes its skin; and, as there is a preference among players for thick heads or thin ones, the thickness must be measured and the head stored in the proper bin.

White calfskin is usually furnished for batter heads of snare drums and for bass drums. This same type of skin, though especially selected for a specific texture, is produced with a transparent finish, instead of cloudy or white, for tympani.

Good tympani heads must be very elastic. The elasticity

of a head, which depends upon its texture, determines what its tone will be. Transparent heads, otherwise known as *clear* heads, are more elastic than white ones, which is the reason they are generally used on tympani. Clear heads stretch and contract more than opaque white ones, and therefore produce a better quality of tone and more resonant volume. Heads that are all white have been made that way by an even stretching during the process of their manufacture. Transparent heads are made from hides in the natural unstretched state; they are, for this reason, more elastic than those that have been stretched, and are better for the snare side of snare drums and for tympani, where maximum vibration is required.

Even with the improved methods of manufacture and increased knowledge acquired relative to the hides of animals, all drumheads are not perfect in every respect. This may be said especially of the heads for kettledrums, for more is demanded of them than of skins for any other kind of drum. Heads for the kettledrums must be as nearly perfect as possible. They must be of the same texture and thickness over their entire surface if perfection is to be even approximated.

The secret of all drumheads, and especially tympani heads, is the *texture* of the grain of the skin from which the head is made. A good head must have flexible grain. It must be resilient. Some heads are cloudy in appearance; they have natural areas of grey or white, or they are mottled with reddish or brown spots, and for this reason are rejected by those who do not know that the appearance of an *unstretched* head has nothing to do with its textural quality nor its tone. The extreme ends of a hide, that portion from the upper neck of an animal, or from the tail, are close-grained and hard, and they will not vibrate in unison with an area that is long-grained and flexible. The long-grained, flexible head of even thickness produces *sustenance,* or longer and richer tones. Unfortunately, most buyers choose drumheads which appeal to their sense of beauty, not knowing that the most attractive head is not necessarily the best one.

Questions relative to the correct thickness of tympani heads are asked quite often. Some prefer thin heads, while others like them thick. Some players use heavier sticks than others. The texture and shape of the sticks used by different players vary greatly. The manner in which the sticks are held, the player's touch in playing, and the pre-conceived mental picture he has of how his drums should sound, all have a definite bearing on his choice of heads. The proper thickness of the head to use is a personal matter, one of individual preference, and one to be govern-ed by the many factors involved.

Thick heads used on kettledrums raise in pitch more rapidly than do thin ones of the same diameter. They have, therefore, more range from low notes to high ones during the same distance of travel by the pedal. For that reason less movement is required when tuning small intervals, — which is not always an advantage.

TUCKING A NEW HEAD, especially one of large size, on a fleshhoop is an operation best assigned to an experienc-ed workman. Large heads are expensive and they are easily ruined. Heads already wrapped on hoops may be purchased from the factory, and this is an advisable method of replacing broken or wornout ones. When this is done, or when new heads are installed on hoops by the mechanic-drummer, care should be taken in having the diametric line which indicates the backbone of the animal as near the exact middle of the drum as possible. This placement is most important for tympani, where tone quality and volume are demanded.

When a new head (mounted on a fleshhoop) is to be installed on a kettledrum, it should be thoroughly dampened up to, but not under the hoop. It should then be allowed to dry for a few moments, or until the head is still quite limp, but not wet. Any extra moisture should then be removed with a dry cloth, and the head (mounted on the hoop) placed on the rim of the drum in such a manner that the diametrical backbone line will run between two opposite tuning handles. This will position the head so the area the drumsticks will strike can be at right angles to the line of the animal's backbone. Theoretically, this is the correct portion of the head on which to play, as the vibrations caused by the touch of the sticks form waves which travel to the center of the drum on the surface of the head, and simultaneously go down and then up the inside of the kettle and repeat the same action from the spot exactly opposite that activated by the sticks. The chief nodes of vibration occur equally on both sides of the diametric line in the head, and if this is placed across the center of the drum the two halves will vibrate equally and be in balance. If the head is a good one, which it may be even though the backbone line is harder in texture than the remainder of the head, it should vibrate evenly on both sides of this line and produce a tone comparative free from falseness *if* all of the six or eight tuning stations are in tune with themselves. In practice, the theory of playing with the sticks at right angles to the backbone line does not always hold true, for occasionally a head will be found to produce its best tone directly on the line. This may be due to some ideosyncrasy inherent in the head, or to some fluke of acoustics; but it is advisable to place this line in a position so it will divide the head into two equal halves, and which will allow the player to strike it at right angles to the line.

As the freshly placed head begins to dry on the drum, tuning to equalize the pitch at each tuning station should begin at once. Tuning the head with itself for a unison should be continued until it has plenty of 'collar,' is fairly dry, and a good tone in the middle register of the drum has been assured.* Several hours should now elapse before the head is actually played upon, for unless it is thoroughly dry it may break from a blow of the drumstick.

After continued use a drumhead may stretch and become false in tone. It sounds dull and dead. It has no volume and it is almost impossible to tune. Tympani heads are prone to suffer in this manner, because it is easier to detect such afflictions on the sensitive kettledrums and to become audibly aware of them. Before discarding a toneless head, or one which has gotten so false that it cannot easi-

---

*The 'collar' of a kettledrum head is that portion of it which extends over the rim of the drum and disappears under the counterhoop and is wrapped around the fleshhoop.

ly be tuned, remove it from the drum (not the hoop), dampen it thoroughly and allow it to dry and shrink for a day or two. When it has dried, dampen it again and re-install it on the drum as if it were an unused new head. If it does not respond favorably to this treatment, the head should be promptly discarded.

If for any reason it becomes necessary to remove the head from a kettledrum, the head should not be re-installed without first having dampened it, for it is almost impossible to install and tune a dry head. This is especially true of a used head which already has a stiff collar established. When a used head is replaced on the drum it should be treated as a new one, and be as carefully tuned and adjusted.

In tuning a head for a unison, the object is to make it *sound* alike at all tuning stations, rather than to put too much importance upon whether the head pulls down equally around its circumference and looks even. Any soft places or variations in thickness or texture in a head will cause it to pull differently at those places, and the unconformaties must be compensated for in the tension regulated at various tuning stations. A head of even thickness and texture will pull down evenly all around the drum and have a good unison; but, nevertheless, the drum should be tuned for *sound*, not for looks.

After the head is thoroughly dry and its initial tuning for unison has become one of never-ending continuity, the best spot for playing on it should be found and marked. Although theoretically this elusive spot should be exactly where the laws of physics indicate it to be on a perfect drumhead, experience shows that this is not always true. The best spot for playing may be between the next two screw-handles, instead of those originally marked, or it may have moved to the opposite side of the drum. The best playing-spot may travel to different places on the head from day to day, or even from hour to hour. The acoustics of different halls, changes in the weather, or different sticks react on the drum and cause the spot to move. It is advisable, therefore, if drums of the revolving type are used, to check them for this best-sounding spot at every opportunity, and to revolve the drum so it will be in the most advantageous playing position.

Changes in atmospheric conditions cause heads to relax or tighten. This upsets the unison of the head, for soft or thin places in a head do not react to changes of humidity at the same rate as do hard or thick places. The drum is then apt to be completely out of tune with itself, and this probability demands that the heads be tested for possible fluctuations in pitch and unisons whenever circumstances permit; for drums are affected more by atmospheric changes than is any other instrument.

Abrupt marked variations of dampness or dryness in the air may cause a kettledrum to change its pitch a fourth or even a fifth in a surprisingly short time. Overhead banks of electric lights which are too near or too hot will dry the air and cause drums to raise their pitch very rapidly. This creates one of the greatest problems of tuning with which the tympanist must contend. Its mate being that of having the outside doors of an auditorium opened during the inter- mission of a concert to reduce the temperature after the hall has been allowed to become hot and dry. This cooling-off process, which usually brings dampness, causes the drums to go flat as rapidly as they previously went sharp.

When tuning kettledrums for a concert they should be tuned to a unison on the most important note each drum is assigned to play during the program and then accept the fact that, due to the texture of the heads or the state of the weather or the acoustics of the hall, the other notes may have to be merely second best. With a fine head, one suited to the player and his surroundings, it is possible to get good tones from the entire range of a drum, if it is tuned properly. But kettledrums are still semi-crude, difficult instruments, and the seemingly endless problems of tune and tone are the faithful companions of every conscientious tympanist.

THE ANCIENT SEARCH for better drum heads still continues, for while these pages are being written, Science has announced a new material from which the heads for drums are being made. As this novel material is almost totally impervious to the weather, it promises a head which will remain constant in pitch. It is of an even thickness, texture and strength, all of which are necessary requirements of a drum head if it is to have a good quality of tone and sufficient volume. It has no diametric line to worry about; and while it seems to be almost unbreakable, it has the virtue of being elastic at the same time. Such heads for either snare drums or tympani are obtainable completely mounted on a fleshhoop, with a suitable collar already established, and this reduces the process of installation to a minimum. This remarkable new material for drumheads is a so-called *plastic*.

While this new scientifically produced substance promises an easily tuned drumhead with a tone free from falseness, one of good quality and surprising volume, only the future can reveal if plastic heads are eventually to replace the traditional ones of skin. Only the future can tell if, after many millenniums of search and experiment, Science has at last come to the aid of primitive man and has given him the answer to his never-ending quest for a better covering for his most fascinating musical instrument.

A Rolled Skin as a Drum.

CHAPTER VII

Tympani Sticks for Kettledrums

EVER SINCE THE first feeling of musical or rhythmical impulses were noticed by the primitive races of mankind, *drumsticks* have shared a place of importance along with that of the drum. Certain traditions or rituals called for special beaters, and besides using his fingers, hands, wrists or elbows, primitive man had also to have different sticks with which to play his drums when the occasion demanded. The shape of the sticks, their size, the material from which they were made, their decorations, all had great significance to the primitive percussionist.

There were hard beaters, semi-hard, and soft. There were long beaters, and short ones. Straight beaters and curved ones. Some with circular ends were made into rattles. There were thick, club-like beaters, and there were thin light ones. Some beaters were tipped with natural rubber. Others had ball-like ends made of skin stuffed with soft padding, such as kapok. Some were more like crude violin bows than they were like drumsticks.

The proper tone of a drum was demanded by the gods and spirits, and the use of an improper stick might nullify the magic power of the drum, or even cause it to make bad magic or bad 'medicine.'

Sometimes wooden clappers were used as drumsticks. At other times rattles became beaters. Some drumsticks were made for special occasions, and then destroyed after being used but once.

The proper drumstick to use often presents a somewhat similar situation to the modern drummer, for the use of sticks that are unsuited to the mood or character of a phrase or a composition may ruin it, even though it is played with technical perfection.

Purcell, Bach, Handel, Gluck, Haydn, Cimarosa, Mozart, Cherubini, Getry and Beethoven! It seems incredible that all these great masters who wrote such wonderful undying music for many generations of musicians and music-lovers past and those yet to come, who wrote so well and so understandingly for the kettledrums, *never heard them played with other than wooden, rubber- or ivory-tipped sticks!* Even Stamnitz, who is said to have 'discovered' the crescendo and diminuendo, and who changed 'piano' from an echo effect to a dynamic color contrasting with 'forte,' never heard the true round velvety tone of the kettledrums. Had Beethoven not become totally deaf in his later years, he might have heard a quality other than the 'blody sounes of battle' produced on the drums for which he wrote so masterfully, for during his lifetime a young French tympanist, Hector Berlioz, began experimenting with various materials from which to make more suitable sticks for the drums.

It was not until the time of Berlioz (1803-1869) that the beautiful resonant tone of the kettledrums was fully recognized and striven for. Berlioz' sticks, according to today's standards, were not much of an improvement over the previous wooden ones. At first Berlioz tried putting leather covers over wooden sticks. This did not satisfy his musical taste, so he tried mushrooms and sponges. Other tympanists joined in the search for better sticks with which to play. Cork balls were placed on handles. Then flannel disks, woolen yarn, lambswool, and at last *felt* in different degrees of density and thickness.

Wood, cork, and yarn were used as cores for the outer covering of the soft balls on the stick handles, and experiments were made with the handles themselves.* Thin sticks were tried, then thick ones. Flexible handles. Stiff ones. Rattan, bamboo, calcutta, whalebone. Ash, birch, cherry, maple. Every imaginable material has been experimented with for tympani sticks, and it is due to Hector Berlioz' being dissatisfied with the unmusical tone produced by hard wooden or ivory sticks, that we are now able to hear the kettledrums as they should sound.

There are, according to Berlioz, three kinds of kettledrum sticks, "the use of which so change the nature of the drum's sound that it is worse than negligence on the part of the composers if they fail to indicate in their scores the kind which they desire the performer to use."

The three kinds listed by Berlioz are those with wooden ends, which "produce a harsh, dry, hard sound; scarcely good for anything but to strike a violent blow, or to accompany a great noise in the orchestra."

---

*It is not only the ball on the playing end of a tympani stick which governs the tone of a drum. The texture and weight of the handles of the sticks, and the way in which the sticks are held, have much to do with the quality of the sound produced.

Then there are "Drumsticks with wooden ends covered with leather," which . . . "are less hard; they produce a sound less startling than the preceding, but they are very dry nevertheless."

In Berlioz' opinion: "Drumsticks with ends of *sponge* are the best, and are those of which the use — musical, rather than noisy — should be more frequent. They give to the kettle-drum a grave, velvety quality of tone, which, making the sounds very neat, renders therefore the tuning very distinct, and suits a large number of gradations soft or loud in execution, wherein the other drum sticks would produce a detestable — or, at least, an insufficient effect."*

Tympani-sticks for the kettledrums have improved greatly since Hector Berlioz became the champion of better sounding drums. While what he had to say relative to the 'detestable effect' of hard sticks is still true, there are very few living tympanists who have ever seen the sponge-headed drumsticks he so earnestly advocated. Fortunately, for the sound of drums, and for music in general, sticks with ends of soft felt have superseded those made with sponges; and hard sticks are now used only for special effects, or by those whose musical taste and appreciation of the beautiful tone of the kettledrums is not all that it should be.

Soon after Berlioz declared war on the 'detestable' wooden sticks and had found a way by which to make the tone of his drums less objectionable,** tympanists began making their sticks with heads of materials other than wood or

*Berlioz, *A Treatise on Modern Instrumentation and Orchestration.* Translated by Mary Cowden Clarke. Permission by Novello & Co., Ltd.
**Wooden sticks produce a superficial percussive sound, which is false in quality, thin in tone, and which has no depth nor body.

ivory, leather, mushrooms or sponges. Small balls of cork ·
were substituted for wooden ones. Later the cork was covered with flannel. Flannel was then cut into several disks
of about an inch in diameter, and fastened to the end of the
sticks by means of two small washer-like 'bone plates'
(buttons), which were held in place by riveting the wooden
end of the stick where it protruded through a hole drilled
in the outer 'plate.' Flannel schlagel (sticks) may be asked
for in some of the older German scores; but the request for
them has, like the sticks, become obsolete.

Eventually lamb's wool, soft yarn, and then felt were
found to be suitable for tympani sticks; and finally, with
the improved soft felt of today, felt has remained in use,
for it is ideal for the purpose. The best grade of soft German felt has been considered the most desirable for the
production of a musical tone, but some American-made felt
is quite acceptable.

After a suitable material was found for the outside covering of the heads of tympani sticks, the inside core for the
felt was given attention and further improvements were
made. Cork formed into thick disks or balls was found to
serve very well for this purpose. Wooden disks or balls
also were good centers for certain sounds, and so was hard
felt or yarn. Each different kind of core, each variation of
thickness and softness of the covering, and the looseness
or tightness with which it was sewed over the core, was
found to produce a different quality of tone. This gave the
player a wide choice when selecting the proper sticks
with which to play, in respect to the mood or character of
a composition and the register of the drum.

Like the double-reed player who finds it impossible to buy reeds to suit him, and who therefore has to make his own, the tympanist must manufacture his own sticks — and do it well — in order to be completely satisfied with this important part of his equipment; for good sticks are hard to find, even in the better drum shops. The choice of sticks, like the choice of heads, is a highly personal matter, and it would be an extraordinary shop wherein one might find sticks to suit the tastes of all players.

Sticks for the kettledrums consist of a handle usually about half an inch in diameter at the butt end, and tapered for nearly two-thirds of its length to approximately five-sixteenths of an inch at the end on which the ball is attached. Most sticks are about thirteen and one-half inches in length. The small playing-ends are sometimes made with a shoulder to accommodate a core of some kind, over which the outside covering of the stick may be fastened. Formerly the handle end of the sticks was furnished with a ball-like knob, and occasionally the score would call for the drums to be played "Mit dem griff."* This meant that the sticks were to be reversed and the wooden ends used on the drums, which is an expedient often used by the tympanist when felt sticks must be changed to wooden ones in a hurry. Such a practice should be resorted to only in emergencies, for the tone produced by the stick handles does not have the sound of real wooden sticks.

The weight and texture of the handle of a stick influences the tone of the drum in addition to the ball attached to its end for playing, and it also controls the *balance* and 'feel'

*"With the handle."

of the stick.

Maple, birch, ash, hickory, white oak or almost any straight, close-grained hard wood is suitable for stick handles. Carefully selected dowels may be used. Calcutta bamboo, being hollow, is lighter in weight than real wood of equal density and diameter, and it is extremely hard and resonant. Although without any noticable taper, it makes excellent handles.

In deference to chronological priority, and owing to the fact that such sticks may be purchased from dealers, the drummer should acquaint himself with wooden sticks.

Holzschlagel, baguettes de bois, or wooden sticks, which once were used on every and all occasions, are now seldom called for; they are, however, a necessary part of the tympanist's collection of beaters. Wooden sticks, usually available in drum shops, may be found in two styles, each with diameters of about seven-eighths of an inch for the knobs used to strike the drum. One kind has ball-shaped ends, while the other has ends shaped like olives. The ball-shaped sticks do not contact as large an area of the drumhead when it is struck as do those shaped like olives, and their handles are apt to be more slender. Ball-shaped heads have a much thinner and more percussive tone than the olive-shaped ones, and they are more likely to break a drumhead. Olive-shaped sticks are usually heavier and stronger. They produce a better tone and more of it. 'Pockets' of soft felt may be fitted over their ends by means of a drawstring, if desired, and they will be found to be very useful sticks.

The best way for acquainting one's self with the task of

making tympani sticks is to very carefully take apart a stick which needs recovering. Particular attention should be paid to the type of stitching that was used originally, and to the direction in which it was sewed. Dental floss is the best material to use for the stitching, as it is fine and at the same time very strong.

Only the best grade of soft piano felt may be used when making sticks, and a seven-sixteenths or one-half inch piece is carefully split into two equal thicknesses. The inner, wooly side of the split felt is used for the outside of the covering. It is measured correctly and sewed with a suitable 'whip' stitch. The ends of the felt will 'gather' when the ends of the dental floss are pulled. The seam across the ball of the stick should be clearly marked with a pencil, for it should always be on the top of the ball when the sticks are in use. If allowed to be on the underneath side of the stick, the seam will produce a clicking sound which will be an extraneous noise disturbing the natural tone of the drum.

Most sticks have a slight warp in them, or at least a certain way of feeling the most comfortable in the player's hands. When this feeling has been established, the outer covering of the ball of the stick should be rotated over the inner core until the pencilled line marking the seam is on top.

Due to hot lights or nervousness, or at times hard work, the player's hands may perspire, and the smooth shiney handles of the sticks become slippery and hard to hold with the relaxed grasp that is so essential to the production of a round, musical tone. In this case the shellac or lacquer finish on the sticks should be scraped off, or adhesive tape may be wrapped around the lower four or five inches of the handle, to prevent the sticks from slipping.

"drums lyke big ketels . . . "

CHAPTER VIII

Orchestral Relationships

ECONOMICALLY, at least, the prime objective of the tympanist is to please the conductor. Ordinarily this consists of playing the printed part exactly as written by the composer, or as it has been 'improved' by the conductor, and in maintaining such deportment and discipline during rehearsals and concerts that would be a credit to the culture and dignity naturally associated with and expected of a fine orchestra.

The tympanist must, of course, consider his or her own artistic urge for expression while interpreting a part, ignoring the audience completely, and complying with never a moment's relaxation to the wishes and musicianship of the conductor. He must also never lose sight of the fact that he, too, is an individual artist; that he must use the part written by the composer, conducted by whoever wields the baton, to express *himself* by producing a musical interpretation of the printed page which conforms to both the composer and the conductor, and which at the same time portrays the imagination and artistry of the *tympanist*.

Actually, in merely playing a part exactly as written, considerable skill is needed. A good conductor expects no less than his own personal idea of perfection, and translating a printed page into the proper musical and emotional sound is no small problem when there are so many factors to contend with, of which the score itself, and perhaps even the conductor, may contribute generously. All that is demanded of the tympanist is that every note be played in its exact rhythmic place; that it is neither too short nor too long, too high nor too low, nor too soft nor too loud; perfectly in tune and in balance, correct in tone, character and timbre, and played with the confidence and grace that is associated with a first-class performance.

It might be of interest to consider some of the various details of the seemingly few requirements needed, so all concerned may have a better understanding of the problems involved.

Probably the most important requirement of the tympanist, from the conductor's point of view, is that he play *with the beat*. The sound of the kettledrums must never be an instant ahead of the beat nor behind it. The tympanist must be extremely and incessantly alert, always following the slightest variation in mood or tempo as indicated by the 'stick,' and always making his playing emulate in sound what the conductor silently beats in the air. At the same time the tympanist must listen to the playing of his colleagues and fit his entrances and figurations with what they are playing, and thereby mold the sound of the orchestra and the beat of the conductor into a grand unit.

Perfection in rhythm, sureness in playing, and the ability to subdivide intricate rhythmic patterns with controlled freedom — flexibility, that is — when necessary, are requirements of the tympanist. No less is acceptable to a first-class conductor.

'Playing with the beat' means that the tympanist must

read the part accurately and play the notes exactly as they are written, counting incessantly, keeping his drums in tune while counting bars rest or while playing, following the most minute indications of the baton, listening attentively to the other instruments, and making each and every entrance with assurance and certainty.

There are other musical obligations and obstacles to be considered, too. Perhaps the part is not all that could be wished for, one not suiting the instruments, poorly written, or confusing. Some tympani-parts look as if they not only were composed at the piano, but that they were intended to be played on a similar keyboard instrument. Many parts look as if they were written mainly to be difficult to play or read. They seem to lack any semblance of musical intent or understanding. Fortunately, these musical conundrums, the sole moronic purpose of which may be that of trying to confuse the conductor as well as the musicians and at the same time disgust genuine music-lovers and turn them away from bonafide concerts, are seldom a seasonal annoyance; for after one or two performances their discordant sounds and freakish rhythms are rightfully relegated to the realm of the silverfish and cobweb, preferably in that long dusty sleep which hath no awakening.

Most tympani-parts are dismally lacking in cues of any sort, either for tuning or playing; and sometimes after cues have been carefully written in for aids, some well-meaning (but grossly misdirected) librarian will 'clean' the part and erase important cues and corrections which may have taken different players several years to incorporate into it, in order to make the part playable.

Playing in tune is no small problem in itself. It is not possible to play in tune unless the drums are adjusted well mechanically and placed to good advantage in the orchestra. The head on each drum must be in tune with itself. It must sound the same pitch at every place on its outer surface. Any falseness in this unison will set up vibrations of unequal length when the head is struck, and this will prevent the production of a clear, vibrant tone. This falseness will also prevent purity of pitch.

One of the difficulties in tuning comes from the fact that drumheads are so sensitive to sympathetic vibration, for even though a drum may be slightly out of tune, it will sound in tune with the other instruments due to some portions of the head vibrating in sympathy with the correct pitch. But let the orchestra stop playing, and the drums play alone! Sympathetic vibration does not help the pitch then, and notes which sounded perfectly in tune but an instant before may sound considerably out of tune when playing unaccompanied.

A tone pure in both pitch and resonance is largely a theoretical hypothesis, however, for heads are seldom of the same thickness and texture all over. Thin places in a head stretch easier than thick places when tension is raised or lowered, and the different rates of vibration given off by areas of unequal thickness will produce a false tone of impure pitch. Continued use of a head will also cause falseness, on account of its stretching and losing elasticity.

Being continuously on the alert and ever listening for flaws in tune and tone, and ever turning his drums in search of a better playing-spot, presents the player of drums with many problems to keep on his mind.

The drums themselves vary in tone production. Some are considerably less vibrant than others, owing to their shape or construction, or to the materials of which they are made. The type of sticks used and the manner in which they are held have a lot to do with the tone of a drum; but a lack of resonance might be due to the acoustics of the hall in which it is being played, or to the weather.*

Soft curtains, draperies, open ceilings, or stage-settings often deaden the tone and make it so false that tuning is very difficult. The vibrations are so nullified and absorbed by nearby soft materials that the volume of tone is greatly reduced, as well.

For a good solid tone, the kettledrums require a good solid floor upon which to rest. The shakey, unsteady floors usually associated with impromptu or portable risers sometimes used for orchestra settings, besides causing a continual tremolo of the musicstands, also reduce the sound of the instruments.

Drumheads are very sensitive, and they re-act eagerly to the principles of sympathetic vibration and to tonal annulment. When placing the kettledrums in an orchestra, this important fact should be considered; for if the drums are placed too near the bass drum, gong, chimes, or harps, they will be subjected to both these phenomena, and unless those instruments are tuned to the same pitch as the tympani they will deaden the vibrations of the latter. If they *are* tuned

*Like those used on other members of the drum family, tympani heads lose elasticity and tone during periods of either very damp or very dry weather. Normal humidity must prevail if a drum is to produce its best quality of sound, its greatest volume, or its purist pitch.

near the same pitch as the kettledrums, it will then be impossible to play short *secco* notes on the drums, for the other instruments will sustain the sound through sympathetic vibration, no matter how quickly the tympanist dampens the drums. This physical reaction is similar to the tuning fork experiment, wherein one fork is activated by the *sound* of another fork of the same frequency of vibration. *Never* place the kettledrums close to soft draperies, chimes, gongs, bass drums, harps, or immediately under open ceilings, if the full roundness and velvety beauty of their tone is desired, if playing in tune is important, or if the proper value of notes is of any consequence.

If the tympanist is to play in balance with the rest of the orchestra, he must be placed near the French horns, trumpets, and trombones; not in the violin section, nor with the clarinets, as is sometimes thoughtlessly or 'unavoidably' done. When placed near the brasses, the tympanist is in close contact with the rhythmic and dynamic sounds of this group of players, his musical rapport will be more easily established and the entire orchestra will benefit. If placed near the more delicate instruments his conscience will not permit him to play as loudly as he should at times. If he is without conscience and plays with a full tone, he will then lose all relationship of balance, for he will not be able to hear anything but his drums. When placed behind the violins or violas, the tympanist suffers (with those around him) whenever the score calls for extreme volume, and the moving bows of the string players distract his attention from the conductor.

In order that the tympanist may more adequately fulfill

the requirements necessary for playing well rhythmically and for following the baton precisely, he must watch the conductor with the utmost attention; for this reason he should have a clear unobstructed view of the conductor at all times. The conductor, in turn, should have sufficient light on himself to be plainly visible to everyone in the orchestra. The light on the conductor should balance with the light on the players' music, in order that the musicians may be able to see him while reading their orchestra-parts and to avoid having to re-adjust the focus of their vision through transferring their attention between their music and the conductor. The conductor should have slightly more light shining on him than the musicians have on their music, for then he is always plainly visible without the necessity of removing eyes from the notes.

Next to having lights shining directly into the musicians' eyes, the greatest source of lighting annoyance is usually caused by the 'teaser.' This is, in theatrical parlance, the curtain which hangs in front of the first bank of overhead lights. Its purpose is to shield these lights so they will not be seen by those sitting in the first few rows of seats in an auditorium; but unless this curtain is properly adjusted *for the orchestra,* as well as for the audience, the conductor is likely to be placed in complete shadow, and he can not be seen by those who are trying to follow his guidance. In such instances really good playing is impossible, for not only must the musicians be able to see the baton, or the conductor's hands, they must also be able to see his *eyes.*

There are certain necessary requirements expected from the conductor, too, if his musicians are to please him. Without these in evidence it is highly improbable that the tympanist (nor anyone else) will be able to do all that is demanded of him. A confidential, *sotto voce* manner of announcing rehearsal numbers, especially those ending in '-een,' or '-ty,' is a source of confusion to an orchestra; for conductors who practice this conservation of speech are habitually swallowing the final words of their announcements, or by ending each sentence with a *molto* diminuendo.

The motion of the conductor's baton is of the greatest importance to the playing of an orchestra, and there are at least three distinct types of conducting which totally demolish the ultimate in symphonic playing — three ways of beating time which are certain to ruin an ensemble.

Probably the least offensive of the three never-failing ways to ruin a performance is the delayed-action technique. This beat is usually preceded by a spectacular 'wind-up,' after which the conductor gives an impressive down-beat. This gymnastic bit seems to be intended for the audience, for the orchestra is not expected to play with its motion, but to take it only as a warning. The actual playing is to begin about half a second after the downward swoop of the baton — the aphelion, as it were — has been delivered. While the preceding delayed-action method of maestronic performance usually occurs at the beginning of a number, another deadly form of this enigmatic style of conducting is sometimes found at the end of a composition or movement when the final sounds of the orchestra are contained in a few detached soft chords. In this case the beat is of a subtle circular character with neither visible beginning nor end, and the desired place in its unintelligible travel for the musicians to play is so vague or esoteric that the resultant tones are apt to remind one of several small soft tuned potatoes being dropped gently at *almost* the same time. A perfect ensemble is not possible with such 'every man for himself' conducting. The players soon learn to disregard the 'beat,' and to rely on their own individual musical sense; but one hundred musical senses on their own initiative in an orchestra do not always provide the best of ensemble playing.

Another unfortunate conductorial affectation is that of the leader who leans toward over-conducting. Each beat and sub-beat has so many frills and rapid rebounds and so much confusion that the actual beat cannot be found. The overall motion is usually carried on in the rhythm being played by the orchestra, but any hope of perfection must be abandoned when confronted by the bouncing-baton technique. The orchestra must have a definite, easily followed beat if it is to play well together.

Undoubtedly the most difficult beat to follow is one which seems to dare the men to play with it. It is never in time with the rhythm of the music, and the player who conscientiously follows the stick will find himself in trouble. Sometimes this *rubato* style of beating time is faster than the rhythmic pulsations, and sometimes it is slower — but it is never with the music. Conductors of this type always seem to have something else on their minds. After a few bars of understandable conducting to get the orchestra started, they relapse into thoughtless out-of-rhythm doodling with the baton, much to the despair of the musicians and to the disappointment of the audience.

Most schooled and experienced conductors of the opera know the importance of conducting or indicating each bar in which their musicians have either notes to play or rests to count; but symphonic maestros sometimes stop beating whenever a solo instrument plays several bars alone. This is especially true in concertos and in vocal arias. Perhaps the soloist will be playing or singing alone or with the accompaniment of one or two sections of the orchestra while the remainder must count almost endless groups of bars rest. Suddenly the conductor stops beating, to resume it again only when some portion of the orchestra has its next entrance; but there are possibly many in the orchestral group whose entrances are later on in the music, and they have no way of knowing where the beating again began, as it occurred somewhere in the midst of their empty bars. If the music librarians have done their duty in the traditional efficient manner and have erased all former cues from the orchestra parts, the entrances to follow will be merely intuitive guesses.

The conductor should indicate each bar of music represented in a composition. Those leaders who have been fortunate enough to have gained experience by playing in an orchestra are not apt to neglect this important bit of musical 'sign posting.'

Grouping three or four bars of swiftly moving music into a phrase, and then beating it as one bar, is extremely confusing to those musicians who habitually watch the conductor. An example of this 'simplified' conducting may sometimes be noticed in the 'Sorcerer's Apprentice,' by Paul Dukas, where three bars of three-eight time (normally conducted one beat to a bar) are beaten as one bar of nine-eight time. The musician who sees the baton swooping far to the right for the *downbeat* of his second bar, and then high in the air for the *downbeat* of his third bar, will find it less distracting if he ignores the conductor entirely, and directs his gaze solely on his music — and silently beats time for himself by clicking his teeth together, or by wiggling his most cooperative big toe.

MUSIC CRITICS have a great deal to do with the success or failure of many conductors and musical organizations, for whatever the critics may say in print is usually blindly accepted as unqualified, absolute truth. Unfortunately, these self-appointed 'authorities' on good or bad in music sometimes suffer from a complex of frustration which permits them to publicize only what, in their often biased or erroneous opinions, they believe to be bad. A good performance is a rare occasion for them to admit. Their objective seems to be to tear down, to destroy rather than to strengthen; to vilify instead of making constructive criticism and encouraging to greater achievement.

Critics have been called by some the 'eunuchs' of Musicdom. As a rule, while being unable to sing or play an instrument themselves, these iconoclastic fault-finders nevertheless enjoy a chronic displeasure from the performance of those who have this enviable ability. A much less destructive method of serving the public *and themselves* would be through criticisms which do not over-emphasize the negative, but which stress the *good* in music or its rendition instead; criticism which would allow them to see the clean white, pearl-like teeth of the dead dog lying by the roadside, instead of only its decaying carcass. Such a humane approach to criticism is not entirely unknown, but it is indeed quite rare. There are some good critics, fair-minded, sincere critics who have a musical background, good taste, and an honest opinion; so it may not be said of all critics, as was once said of the Indian, that the good ones are only the dead ones.

In their appraisal of performances, music critics often tell of orchestras being un-rehearsed or of having an 'off' night, on occasions of poor playing or bad conducting. The possibility of the conductor's beating having some bearing on the quality of a concert is a matter seldom considered. If the performance is good, the credit goes to the conductor; if it is bad, the fault lies with the orchestra. 'The stick can do no wrong' seems to be an accepted opinion of the critics; yet, in the words of the immortal maestro Arturo Toscanini, "The baton means nothing without the orchestra. The orchestra and the conductor share equally in a good performance."

Not many years ago a concert was given at Hollywood Bowl in which the program consisted of Leonore Overture Number Three, and the Ninth Beethoven Symphony. The conductor was sadly paralysed and was barely able to stand alone. He could not move his right hand at all, and had but the slightest use of his left hand, with which he tried to conduct. There was scarcely enough motion in his beat to vaguely indicate the time to start playing. There was no actual conducting at all. Yet the men and women of the orchestra, through deference and pity for the conductor who had seen far better — and more imperious — days, worked like they never had worked before, and the result was a fine concert in spite of the serious handicap.* Needless to say, it was the non-conducting conductor who was given credit and praise for the splendid performance. The orchestra was given no consideration nor appreciation for its part in a most generous gesture. But it did demonstrate that perhaps it might sometimes be better to have no conductor at all, than to have one whose abstract gyrations are likely to upset the orchestra.

First of all, the conductor should provide a good beat. One that leaves little to the imagination, and which is not easily misunderstood. A *good* beat is one that is up when it should be, and down when it should be. It should not be filled with fanciful ornamentations, intricate embellishments, nor should it be too circular in character. The up-beat should always set the tempo which follows. The beat

---

*This same conductor, only a few short seasons before, refused one of the orchestra members permission to be excused from an unimportant rehearsal in order that he might attend his mother's funeral. The date of the funeral had to be changed so it would not interfer with the rehearsal schedule. Another conductor, *requiescat in pace*, openly declared that he would shoot any musician in the orchestra who might make a serious mistake during a concert, and he boasted about carrying a revolver in his pocket for that special purpose.

Many conductors, on account of their outstanding musicianship, human qualities or personal charm, fortunately enjoy the love and respect of the members of their orchestra; but even when this desirable relationship is non-existent, the orchestra will not intentionally give less than its very best efforts and artistry when playing a concert, no matter what its personal feelings toward the conductor may be.

should be clearly subdivided for complicated figurations in slow tempo. All important entrances should be cued, and ample time should be allowed for tuning or the turning of pages between movements or compositions played during a concert.

The conductor, as well as the tympanist, should know the proper sound the kettledrums should produce, and both conductor and tympanist should strive for a tone similar to the beautiful round tone of a fine resonant Stradivarius 'cello or double-bass played pizzicato by a great artist, rather than like savages pounding on tom-toms with sticks made from the gnawed bones of their departed enemies — unless such a scene is intended.

The conductor should not intimidate with speech, nor damn with looks those who are striving to please his every whim, for in doing so he will only make bad matters worse. Unthinking conductors sometimes defeat their own ends by making their musicians so nervous that they 'freeze' and cannot do justice to themselves, the music, nor to the conductor. First-class musicians have been ruined or even actually killed by the treatment they have received from their leader. The Me-and-god attitude in a conductor is one that is highly unsatisfactory, if cooperation and good music are to be achieved. Fortunately, this type of conductor has become a *rara avis*. A smile, or a glance of assurance, goes a long way to create a fine performance.

If the conductor will give some consideration to the problems of the tympanist, and understand him and his instruments, he will find the kettledrums his greatest ally in the orchestra. If he will *lead* instead of drive, inspire his men instead of curtailing their abilities, then and then only will he be able to achieve greatness as a conductor and respect as a man; for then and then only will it be possible for his men to contribute their part in making his career a success.

The Sutri-nahabat, my friend,
Brings up the rear — this is the end.

BIBLIOGRAPHY

Arizona State Teachers' College, *Arizona*
    Hastings House, New York   1940
John D. Baldwin, *Prehistoric Nations*
    Harper & Brothers, New York   1896
Hector Berlioz, *A Treatise on Modern Instrumen-*
    tation and Orchestration, translated by
    Mary Cowden Clarke.
    Novello & Co., Ltd., London, England   1882
Mary E. and William Adam Brown, *Musical*
    Instruments in Their Homes
    Dodd, Mead & Co., New York   1888
Charles L. Camp, *The Earth Song*
    University of California Press, Berkeley   1952
Ruben M. Campos, *El Folklore y la Musica*
    Mexicana
    Publicaciones de la Secretaria de
    Educacion Publica, Mexico   1928
John F. Carrington, *Talking Drums of Africa*
    Carey Kingsgate Press, London   1949
Col. James Churchward, *The Children of Mu;*
    The Lost Continent of Mu
    Ives Washburn, New York   1931
E. Colbert, *Humanity in its Origin and Early Growth*
    Open Court Publishing Co., Chicago, Ill.   1892
Sadis N. Coleman, *The Drum Book*
    The John Day Co., New York   1931
Leonard Cottrell, *The Anvil of Civilization*
    New American Library, New York   1957

Frances Densmore, *The American Indians and
Their Music*
The Woman's Press, New York   1936
Ignatius Donnelly, *Atlantis*
Harper & Brothers, New York   1882
Will Durant, *Our Oriental Heritage*
Simon & Schuster, New York   1954
Beatrice Edgerly, *From the Hunter's Bow*
G. P. Putnam's Sons, New York   1942
Louis C. Elson, *Curiosities of Music*
Oliver Ditson & Co., Boston   1880
Rodney Gallop, *Music of Indian Mexico;*   1939
Otomi Indian Music from Mexico   1940
Schirmer, New York
Delia Goetz and Sylvanus G. Morley (from the
Spanish Translation by Adrian Recinos)
*Popul Vuh, The Sacred Book of the Ancient
Quiche Maya*
University of Oklahoma Press, Norman, Okla.   1950
William K. Gregory, *Our Face from Fish to Man*
G. P. Putnam's Sons, New York   1929
Victor W. van Hagen, *Realm of the Incas*
New American Library of World
Literatures, Inc., New York   1957
Handbook of South American Indians
United States Government Printing Office,
Washington, D.C.   1948
Ernest Albert Hooton, *Apes, Men, and Morons*
G. P. Putnam's Sons, New York   1937
Thomas Henry Huxley, *On the Man-like Apes*

J. M. Dent & Sons, Ltd., London 1910

Thomas Athol Joyce, *Maya and Mexican Art*
 The Studio, Ltd., London 1927

Percival R. Kirby, *Musical Instruments of the
 Native Tribes of South Africa* 1930
 The Kettledrums 1934
 Oxford University Press, London

Kroeber, *Anthropology*
 Harcourt, Brace & Co., New York 1948

Kyung Lin Song, *Graceful Music of Korea*
 Office of Public Information, Republic of
 Korea, Seoul 1959

Harold Lamb, *Genghis Khan, The Emperor of
 All Men*
 Garden City Pub. Co., Garden City, N. Y. 1927

Earl Leaf, *Isles of Rhythm*
 A. S. Barnes & Co., New York 1948

Prince John Lowenstein, *A Bronze Kettledrum
 (T'ung-ku) in the Eu Collection*
 Journal of the Malayan Branch Royal Asiatic
 Society, Singapore, Malaya 1958

Wm. F. Ludwig, Sr., *Complete Drum Instructor*
 Wm. F. Ludwig Drum Co., Chicago, Ill. 1942

Samuel Marti, *Instrumentos Musicales Pre-
 cortesianos*
 Instituto Nacional de Anthropologia, Mexico 1954

Bernard S. Mason, *Drums, Tom-toms, Rattles*
 A. S. Barnes, New York 1938

D'Arcy McNickle, *They Came Here First*
 J. B. Lippincott Co., New York 1949

Dr. John Ballou Newbrough, *Oahspe*
 Kosmon Press, Los Angeles and London   1935
Henry Fairfield Osborn, *Men of the Old Stone Age*
 Charles Scribner's Sons, New York   1948
The Travels of Marco Polo (The Venetian)
 Revised from Marsden's Translation and
 Edited with Introduction by Manuel Komroff
 Boni & Liveright, New York   1926
Hugh Miller, *The Old Red Sandstone*
 J. M. Dent & Sons, Ltd., London   1906
George Prentiss, *Ages of Ice and Creation*
 Common Good Press, Chicago, Illinois   1915
G. de Purucher, *Studies in Occult Philosophy*
 Theosophical University Press,
 Pasadena, California   1945
Ettie A. Rout, *Maori Symbolism*
 Kegan Paul, Trench, Truber & Co., Ltd.
 London   1926
Curt Sachs, *The History of Musical Instruments*
 W. W. Norton & Co., Inc., New York   1940
Andrew V. Scott, *Drumology*
 Wm. K. Smith Music Company, New York   1940
G. C. Vaillant, *The Aztecs of Mexico*
 Penguin Books, Ltd., Middlesex, England   1950
Charles Villiers and Cecil Forsyth,
 A History of Music
 The Macmillan Company, New York   1925
Robert Stevenson, *Music in Mexico*
 Thomas Y. Crowell Co., New York   1952
Edwin Way Teale, *Boys' Book of Insects*

E. P. Dutton & Co., New York   1940
The World Book Encyclopaedia
    W. F. Quarrie & Co., New York   1943
William H. Worrel, *A Study of the Races in the
    Ancient Near East*
    Appleton & Company, New York   1927
H. S. K. Yamaguchi, *We Japanese*
    Fujiya Hotel, Miyanoshita, Hakone, Japan   1950

SCHEDULE OF SUBJECTS